# What We Can Learn From The Animals About Office Politics

Dr Michael Teng

Published in December 2008 by
Corporate Turnaround Centre Pte Ltd.

Printed in Singapore
by Markono Print Media Pte Ltd.

9  8  7  6  5  4  3  2
09

ISBN   978-981-08-1940-8

---

**Copyright @ Dec, 2008 by Corporate Turnaround Centre Pte Ltd.**
All rights reserved. This publication is protected by Copyright and permission should be obtained from the publisher prior to any prohibited reproduction, storage in a retrieval system, or transmission in any form or by any means, electronic, mechanical, photocopying, recording, or likewise. For information regarding permission(s), write to: admin@corporateturnaroundcentre.com

*What We Can Learn From The Animals About Office Politics*

*Playing in the Concrete Jungle without being Played Out During Global Economic Recession*

Table of Contents

    Table of Illustrations..................................................................................i

    Introduction..............................................................................................ii

    Background of the Author..................................................................... iv

I. Are office politics really that bad?......................................................1

II. What makes you think you can escape the office politics jungle?........................22

III. Office Politics in Person-to-Person Interaction………………………………31

IV. When the State of the Office Influences Action……………………….. 48

V. Five Ways to Succeed – Becoming King of the Jungle …………………………62

VI. Five Ways to Fail – What the animals can tell us to avoid ……………………74

VII. Fight or Flight – When to put up your dukes or cut and run …………………..90

VIII. The Human Animal – Our Innate Good and Bad Animal Instincts ……………98

IX. A Favorite Animal – How choosing one can help you ……………………….116

X. When Nothing Stays the Same – How to deal with transition …………………123

XI. Appropriate Action – A summary of the lessons we can learn ……………….135

# Table of Illustrations

| Illustration | Page Number | Illustration Number |
|---|---|---|
| Office of Clueless People | 1 | 1 |
| Out For Lunch | 4 | 2 |
| Lioness Preening | 8 | 3 |
| Rats for Hire | 14 | 4 |
| Vacuuming/Walking Dog/ Working | 23 | 5 |
| Snake Eating Man | 25 | 6 |
| Gazelles Fighting Over Girl | 33 | 7 |
| Lion and Hyena Dinner | 35 | 8 |
| Hard-Working Beaver | 40 | 9 |
| Monkey Teams | 41 | 10 |
| Shark Dinner | 44 | 11 |
| Jungle Surgery | 50 | 12 |
| Chameleon | 61 | 13 |
| Arm Wrestling in Office | 62 | 14 |
| Lion Marking His Territory | 66 | 15 |
| Peacock with the Ladies | 68 | 16 |
| Sad Panda | 80 | 17 |
| Hard-Working Bird | 82 | 18 |
| Deer Being Hunted | 89 | 19 |
| Lion in Bath / Shark Out of Water | 91 | 20 |
| Monkey-baby Toy Taking | 102 | 21 |
| Monkey-baby Biting | 108 | 22 |
| Mustang Rearing | 117 | 23 |
| Mustang is the Lion's Dinner | 122 | 24 |
| Lion is Afraid of Snakes | 124 | 25 |
| Elephant Listening for Typhoon | 128 | 26 |
| Wise Man | 3, 20, 43, 46, 63, 65, 94, 109, 143 | 27 |

i

## **Introduction**

The animal world is rife with office politics and through simple observations, we can see how animals react to the same situations we find in the concrete jungle. The animals play politics as a way of life to survive in the jungle. And if they get played out, it may mean ending up as a meal for other animals. By making comparisons to the animal world, we can increase our toolbox of tactics to succeed in our offices. During these days of global economic slowdown, the political fight for job preservation becomes more intense, the ability to handle office politics is even more critical.

This is the rationale for writing this book. With the global recession, many jobs are going to be lost, and our concrete jungle is quickly becoming a true struggle for survival of the fittest. In these conditions, performance is not enough. By learning from animals which meet crisis frequently and observing how they survive we can increase our own ability to survive in the concrete jungle.

This book is universal because as long as there are people, notwithstanding the culture, there are politics. We each must deal with people's egos, backgrounds and motivation (along with many other individual issues) and as jobs retrenchment increases and companies go bust, the fight for job preservation and survival becomes increasingly intense. The animal behavior in us surfaces in these circumstances. And when our animal behavior increases, so does the tendency toward survival of the fittest.

When this type of behavior takes precedence in the concrete jungle, everybody must wise-up and perform, otherwise he or she will not keep their job for very long. But simple performance under such circumstances is not enough. One needs to excel and stand out among the crowd - thus playing the political game well is critical.

But playing well does not mean playing dirty. By no reach of imagination is this book espousing playing dirty politics. Animals do not do that and nor is it natural for humans to do so. Animals do not play the political game out of malice or greed. They play the game to protect themselves and their young. Even predators do not kill for killing's sake. Once these predators have their fill, they leave the other prey-animals alone until the next meal. The animal ecosystem is a fair and balanced world that has lasted for millennia.

This delicate balance based on ethical politics is why we do not see the systemic collapse of the animal kingdom as we are currently seeing in our economic system. The biggest destruction in the animal kingdom is actually caused by men who are invading into then animals' space, polluting the environment and the air and hunting animals ruthlessly for private gain. Because of their delicate balance, the animals even survive the destructive forces of Mother Nature such as drought and famine. But many species of animals are destroyed by men. It is in our best interest to learn from the animals and form this same balance in our lives to better survive in the concrete jungle.

## Background of the Author

Dr. Mike Teng is the author of a best-selling book "Corporate Turnaround: Nursing a sick company back to health," in 2002 which is also translated into the Bahasa Indonesia. In 2006, he authored another book entitled, "Corporate Wellness: 101 Principles in Turnaround and Transformation." He also published in 2007/2008 five management books, namely entitled: "Internet Turnaround: The Use of Internet Marketing to Turnaround Companies;" "Training Manual: Corporate Turnaround and Transformation Methodology;" "Link Baiting to Improve Your Page Ranking on Search Engines" and "Corporate Turnaround: Global Perspective as well as Fundamentals of Buying and Selling of Companies."

Dr. Teng is currently the Managing Director of Corporate Turnaround Centre Pte, Ltd. which provides corporate training and management advisory services. He has 28 years of experience in corporate turnaround, strategic planning and operational management responsibilities in the Asia Pacific. Of these, he held Chief Executive Officer's positions for 18 years in multi-national and publicly listed companies.

Dr. Teng served as the Executive Council member for fourteen years and the last four years as the President of the Marketing Institute of Singapore (2000 – 2004), the national marketing association. Dr. Teng holds a Doctor in Business Administration (DBA) from the University of South Australia, Master in Business Administration (MBA) and Bachelor in Mechanical Engineering (BEng) from the National University of Singapore. He is also a Professional Engineer (P Eng, Singapore), Chartered Engineer ( C Eng, UK) and Fellow Member of several prestigious professional institutes namely, Chartered Institute of Marketing (FCIM), Chartered Management Institute (FCMI), Institute of Mechanical Engineers (FIMechE), Marketing Institute of Singapore (FMIS), Institute of Electrical Engineers (FIEE) and Senior Member of Singapore Computer Society (SMSCS).

### Are office politics really *that* bad?

Do you ever wake up in the morning, visions of angst and uncomfortable office moments swimming in your head? Has some situation in the office ever gotten you so worked-up that you couldn't sleep? If you don't want to admit it, that's ok. I'll admit it for you. I've certainly felt this way and I would bet that you have, too.

No matter how long or short we have been in our careers, we have each learned that it is a constant struggle to succeed in the marketplace. And while you are busy trying to muddle-through, so is everyone else around you! And the best part – as we each make our ways through the world, none of us really has any idea what we're doing!

> *If we're all muddling-through and have no idea what we're doing – maybe we should acknowledge this failing and learn to work with it instead of against it.*
>
> Illustration 1

1

We can see that we're each struggling to win by looking at the politics that are being played in the American Congress regarding the approval of the economic bailout. Although the whole world might collapse without this bailout, the legislators are bickering and arguing, fussing and jockeying for position. And while they negotiated for pork-barrel additions to a critical issue, the world held its breath – and Congress never realized that not making a decision was making the worst decision of all! This is a prime example of how politics can overtake rational thinking. Although the final decision was made to approve the 700 USD billion rescue plan – it was too little too late. The Dow Jones and global stock markets continued to plummet as they lost confidence in the US authority's ability to solve the financial crisis.

However, with knowledge comes power. By remembering to think before we act (or in Congress's case, thinking before not acting), we can keep ourselves from falling into that trap. By keeping our wits about us, we can survive and actually thrive within the confines of this crazy politically-charged world!

Because the office environment really is "survival of the fittest" with a vicious and brutal lifecycle just like those boring books in science class described, keeping our wits about us in this setting is critical. And the pressure to do this has become more urgent in the face of the recent global economic downturn. This has led many people to consider just how to best survive in this coming time which has already been rife with layoffs, mergers and general turmoil. After some very intriguing observations, I learned that there are some very strong similarities between the jungle and our offices. And that made me ponder the possibility that we might be able to learn some tricks from the animals to face the political game on our daily forays into the concrete jungle. Animals face crisis or the threat of crisis everyday – from drought, famine, flood, forest fires to even being eaten alive if they're not careful enough. Animals have learned to cope with their own brand of office politics, honing their behavior into a fine art of specialization for the survival of each of their species.

*Man's enemies are not demons, but human beings like himself.*

*~ Lao Tzu*

Illustration 27

Based on my review of the television shows which proudly show us the mean-streets of the animal world, the jungle is an integrated ecosystem and each animal is an integrated part of that system. Surprisingly, our office environments are based on the same principles! So, it's pretty easy to deduce that the environments in which we work are integrated office-ecosystems and each person is an integrated part of that system. Just take a look at your own office. Do you think you could do your job well if your administrative assistant decided to stop helping you? And do you think that your boss could do his job well if you were busy focusing on the duties of the administrative assistant? And if this anarchy were to occur, how many other people would be affected by your inability to focus on your core-duties?

I know that in my own situation, there would be a great number of people that would be unable to complete most of their core-functions if I were to suddenly shutdown. And it is this intricate system upon which we have become so reliant. Think about your home-life. Do you work in partnership with your spouse or significant other? Or do you hire someone to help with your household chores? Either way, you have an intricate system which helps you to efficiently and effectively manage even your home-life.

*If you are perpetually "out for lunch," how many people are affected – how big is the network around you? And imagine all those which you are dependent on – how would you deal if they were all "out to lunch."*
Illustration 2

One can even look to the news reports and the events which overtook the economic scene in America in 2008. Wall Street collapsed under the weight of poor political and regulatory choices. Just to point-out a few of the big examples, we can see from the collapse of Bear Stearn, Lethman Brothers, and AIG that we created an intricate network of intertwined connections which could easily be described as an economic or political ecosystem. And the effects of these collapses are resounding throughout the lives of every man, woman, and child – and especially the office environment. Because of the substantial changes in the economic environment, changes in the office environment have already begun to occur.

In the mid and later parts of 2008, several firms, although extremely financially stable and still showing a substantial profit, have begun downsizing, restructuring, relocating headquarters, and creating a virtual bloodbath within the office. In this type of situation, the mentality of "survival of the fittest" is becoming more and more prevalent. In these tough times, performing well is only the first step – playing the political game will be the key element that can ensure survival. And the solution to this economic crisis will be quite a time in coming, perhaps even years. Even as we struggle now to change our economic policies and governments create 700-billion dollar packages, the solution lies at the basis of the problem – the world's dependence on oil, inflation, short-sighted decisions within major financial firms. It's a virtual economic war out there!

So, how does this all fit-in with our story? Well, that's simple. Since we're all interconnected, it would make sense that the war is not only in our stock markets, the lending markets affected by Freddie Mac and Fannie Mae, or the far-away world of Wall Street but also here in our own backyard. If we are vigilant and take on our small part in the war with a vengeance, we can become part of the solution. If we can foster innovation within our individual firms by playing the political game and striving to be the very best we can be, our part of the world will be improved by that much. Just because the world is going crazy doesn't meant that we can't think rationally and help ourselves be a head above the rest.

*Playing the Political Game is a Part of Life*

If we have to get out of our comfy beds, shower, eat breakfast, climb into our cars and open those doors to the office every morning, then office politics are just a way of life we have to learn to live with. I did this same thing every day for many years, struggling with everyone else until I began to think about my situation and how I might change myself to a better deal. And as a study in helping myself become more successful, I took a look at how the animals successfully play within their version of the concrete jungle every day. I have been applying these techniques for quite some time and have found them to be very effective in our daily interactions. And I find this to be true, because just like us humans, animals are inherently political, if in their own way.

They are political because each animal, big and small, predator and victim, etc. has a role to play and is able to live harmoniously with all the other animals in the same jungle. You have predators, prey and a lot of interaction between the two, sure, but the cycle of life continues. If we can harness some of the innate knowledge and coping skills that the animals have, we might just learn how to play our own game more successfully. Because that's what this story is – playing the political game more successfully than ever before. Learning a bit more about how to handle ourselves and how to deal with other people by seeing how our animal brethren deal with similar situations could give us a few more tools with which to navigate the office world.

I do not suggest that we each sit in front of the television for hours watching animal-lovers-shows trying to divine the way of animals. However, I do implore each person reading this book to think critically about the animal behavior you are already familiar with and how their interactions might be similar to those we have with each other. Because people come from the animal world and the animals have much that they can teach us. Even if you believe that we were created by the hand of God, it is hard to deny that at one time, we did live in the same jungle as the animals. So, surely, they and we share some of the same innate behaviors that come from the same place – our instincts.

And as you read this book remember that there are people of every type, shape and ability, the same as our animal counterparts. Each person has a role to play just like the animals. And not everyone will understand exactly how each animal or each person plays, but I assure you that they do. And because 50% of our population is make-up of the female-type, similar to the animals, keep in mind that the women within your organization (including those of you reading this that are women) are an integral part of the office-ecosystem.

We should acknowledge that women have an important position within the corporate world, just as the lioness' role is crucial to the survival of the lion-species. Because, surely, if the lioness was not there, nor could the lion exist, and likewise for any female counterpart of any species. We are all important in our way and should be recognized as such. But we should all remember that survival to the females of any species is somewhat different and rife with different dangers than that of the male portion of the species.

*The lioness is also a lion – and can be king of the jungle in her own way, but must be aware that there are different dangers in the wild jungle for her.*
*Illustration 3*

Women must tread lightly in the concrete jungle – there are many reasons why a woman may be in a situation where her job would be in jeopardy because of her gender. While men are rarely harassed by other men, women may often be in a room full of men and, although it is not intentional, one or more of the men may join-in on a joke which is inappropriate for mixed company. Although a woman may interpret this type of behavior as sexual harassment, it is an undefined difference. If this same woman were to make a statement about the inappropriateness of the joke, she may be shunned and seen as a whiner.

However, every woman should be aware that sexual harassment exists and can truly affect one's career – the choice of whether or not to cry foul is one each woman may face in her career. Even woman-to-woman sexual harassment may occur. Take my friend Terri for example.

*Tao's Story*

Tao had worked for Heng for only a month when Heng started inviting her to lunch. Tao didn't think anything of the invitations or that Heng paid – Heng's salary was significantly more than Tao's, so she thought it was alright. When Tao had been there for about three months, Heng brought Tao a gift – a lawnmower. This was very convenient as Tao's had just malfunctioned and was unable to be repaired. Tao was so grateful; she still didn't suspect that anything might be inappropriate.

Even when Heng bought Tao a coat as the weather turned colder, Tao didn't consider that Heng might think more of their relationship than Tao suspected. It was when Tao started dating a guy in the building next door that things turned sour. Heng began berating Tao by e-mail for minor mistakes and imagined problems, even yelling at her in front of the entire office for a mistake that Heng made herself! Then Heng began threatening Tao's job and the executive officer had to step-in and keep Tao from being fired. Tao only began to suspect Heng was romantically interested in her after Heng demoted Tao and then left the firm. Tao's demotion held a significant pay decrease and reduction in responsibility – all because she didn't notice that her female boss was interested in her. Imagine if things might have been different if Tao hadn't thought about the possibility earlier-on that Heng was romantically interested.

I know that this sounds like an unlikely event. However, it may happen more than we know. And even man-to-woman sexual harassment may happen more than we know. It's a tough call for a woman to speak-out against harassment, but it is something that may have to be done to save one's career.

And I have found that it is ok to speak-out anonymously or through whistle blowing program if you see this type of behavior occurring in your workplace even if you aren't involved. It certainly didn't bother me when Nico, the Information Technology Director in my office started buying gifts for a young lady in my group named Mee. And I would never have thought twice about it – maybe they were dating, right? Wrong. When I overheard Mee one day speaking to a co-worker about the situation and how uncomfortable she was, but also how afraid she was to speak-out against a director, I knew it was in everyone's best interest if I stepped-in. Now, it was not my place to go speak directly to Nico, but I did go talk to the Human Resources Director. When I explained the situation, immediate action was taken. And Nico didn't lose his job, but neither did Mee lose any face. And no one but the Human Resources Director and I know who made the complaint!

However, some women may find their jobs in jeopardy for quite the opposite situation. If a woman chooses to utilize their gender to achieve favoritism or power, she can be quickly removed from her position. Even if a woman is not intentionally playing to her sex, she may be labeled the same – and this can come from not only the men in the office but also the other women. Jin was a young lady in my office recently which learned this lesson very well.

*Jin's Story*

Jin wasn't trying to impress anyone. She was an administrative assistant in a large office with plenty of much younger and more attractive ladies. And because there were so many young ladies that dressed younger than Jin, she decided that she should also start dressing younger.

Unfortunately, Jin chose clothing that was too provocative and too revealing. Her pants were too tight and her breasts were near to bursting from her shirts. Soon, none of the women in the office would talk to her except when absolutely necessary – and the men were talking to her all too often without any need. Her boss soon noticed that she was getting less and less work done and her relationships with the other administrative assistants were suffering because they would no longer work with her. Rather than confronting the issue, her boss deflected and transferred Jin to another office. When she couldn't find a workable situation at her new office, she was fired.

Generally, the message is for women to understand that they play a significant role in the corporate jungle – but there are significant pitfalls that lay in wait. Women need to be aware of the danger and be cautious at all times to ensure that they are not the focus of traditional gender issues, or the emerging issues that may be unique to their situation. However, women have the potential to do just as well as men, given that they avoid the pitfalls and maintain a proactive approach to advocating their careers. We need to keep in mind that women are half of the population – with half of the brainpower.

Keep in mind also that we can learn from any animal, no matter what their label in our society. For example, think about the brave little rat. Rats have been on this planet for a very, very long time. They have outlived the dinosaurs and have infiltrated most of the known planet. While considered poorly in many cultures, some rats (cute white ones, mostly) are used in the laboratory for medical tests because their genes are similar to the human. In several countries, some rats are considered food and are a rich and healthy source of proteins. However, bad rats and mice are often regarded as pests because they can carry disease, they get into our food and they are everywhere.

Once someone is labeled as a pest in their organization, it is very difficult to change the perception. Everyone within an office talks, so everyone will know. Because of the danger that a political pest presents, people are wary and will react poorly when interaction is necessary with that person. This is true even with change of management. New managers talk with the staff and quickly get a feel for the office environment. And as quickly as they determine who the political pests are, they will single them out for termination or avoid them. Hence the rationale for playing fair at all times in the political game. And the pressure to do this is increasing with the increase in economic difficulty and turmoil. If you are caught playing dirty politics in tough times, you can be sure that you will be played out.

People can be fooled once or twice or brush-off a political no-no as a mistake, but repeated offenses are quickly noted. Once a person has crossed the line to the pest label, carrying the disease of unethical and immoral politics, the perception is nearly impossible to change – people can accept weaknesses if performance is poor, but once a supervisor cannot trust the integrity of an employee and finds that they are a pest, it is very difficult to unravel. People see quickly who is playing bad politics and will quickly brand those people as pests – including bosses and supervisors. Bad politics may include lying and cheating, character assassinations and other unwholesome games to usurp power, etc. This is because you can only practice dirty politics once or at the most twice and you will be quickly found out and branded as a pest. Either you will be condemned forever or you will be fired if caught for playing such malicious games. So, although we can learn from the strong survivability of the rat, we can also learn from the rat that playing dirty politics can brand you for life as a pest and leave you without any ability to survive the office jungle!

*If you become a rat, beware the consequences – often rats may find themselves used and looking for another job with all the other rats.*
Illustration 4

This is a lesson that cannot be stressed enough. Those who play dirty politics will eventually die by the sword. Playing unethically in the office has the same results as playing dirty politics on the world political stage. The election saga of Anwar Ibrahim in Malaysia is a good example of the backlash that is generated when unethical politics are played. In Malaysia, the Barisan Nasional (BN) party under Dr Mahathir accused Anwar Ibrahim, the candidate of the opposition party of sodomy, arrested him and tried to paint him as an immoral villain. However, the voters clearly saw through the desperate ploy and voted near unanimously for Anwar, making him the leader of the Malaysian opposition.

However, we're not here to talk the world political stage (although it makes great examples). We're here to talk real-corporate examples. So, here's one. It's about an acquaintance of mine, Aiko, who couldn't wait to get to the top, so much so that he started playing dirty and his survival was very much in question.

*Aiko's Story*

Aiko had approached the work world with avarice and attacked it as if it were prey and he the predator. He earned his way to the top, attaining an executive position working with a firm he had dreamed of working with throughout his career. Aiko was so happy with his position and his rise to power was so quick, he missed a critical lesson – ethics. When it came time to assign contracts to consultants, he chose those firms in which he had invested his personal money or which were run by his close friends.

The local news media learned that although Aiko had never taken a bribe, he had given lucrative contracts to his friends and firms in which he had invested. The stories were all over the news media for several weeks. Aiko's board of directors fired him within a month, releasing the contracts he had signed and hiring a new executive officer before Aiko even realized exactly what was going on.

In Aiko's situation, it is clear to see that unethical office politics is truly unacceptable. Perhaps Aiko could have made his ascent to the top, albeit a little slower but held onto it for much longer if only he had played clean politics and kept all the dealings "above the table."

Likewise, an animal which steps outside of the bounds of their role is either eaten, shunned from their group and therefore doomed to death, or starved for lack of food. This is the case with the king of the jungle – the lion. If a young male takes it into his mind to attack the leader of the group or takes advantage of the females when they do not wish to mate, the older male will often chase the young male from the den, forcing it into a life of solitude and possible starvation. Even monkeys, our closest animal-relative, will cast-out a member if they are too forward with the female monkeys, steal young or food, or even if they simply step outside of the appropriate behavioral patterns.

To sharpen this point, we can look to the snake. The snake is the most despicable player within the jungle. Not only do they prey on the young, old and defenseless animals, they sneak and steal resources from other animals. They do not protect their young and are vicious creatures. Snakes will sneak into another animal's den such as the prairie-dog and not only eat the young, but will take the den for its own, leaving the prairie-dog with no shelter. Snakes have also been known to eat their young, kill their mates, and attack each other without regard to the social behavior that other species exhibit. As a result, the snake leads a solitary life, meeting other snakes only during the mating season and avoiding all contact except with their meals.

Similarly, there are those people who hog resources for themselves, lie, cheat and steal – clawing their way to the top without a thought for the others around them. These people not only bring disrespect and enmity to themselves, but also to the firm at which they work. Not only do bosses know these snakes in the grass, customers know them too. And snakes don't survive in the same skin very long – they are always shedding their skin and thereby making themselves vulnerable. The people who portray the snake in the concrete jungle are always in the process of having to shed their skins and often will find themselves in hostile situations from which they cannot survive and thus lose their jobs. Imagine continually having to switch roles and re-invent oneself on a near-continual basis. What an abysmal life that would be.

Yes, sometimes office politics are unsavory, but playing is required if you want to survive, especially in a recession environment. All you must do is look around yourself at those who have gone before you or are with you now in the office-ecosystem and see the truth: if you don't play the political game, you get played out and you won't survive.

Think about the last person who was passed-over for a promotion. Maybe it's you or someone you know. Maybe it's just someone who you heard about. What did they do wrong? I bet if you took a very honest look at the situation, you would find that the person that lost out on the promotion, performance being equal, is simply not as good at playing office politics as the one that was promoted. If you desire to move up in your organization and defy the difficult economic times by keeping your career on-track, playing the political game is critical.

Keep in mind that the need to succeed exists throughout a career, however during times of a particularly stressed economy, this need becomes far more paramount to maintaining one's employment. In economically difficult times, corporations have to tighten belts and trim the fat to help stabilize their own operations. They may do this through price increases to consumers, or reductions of overhead expenses, but most often, corporations trim budgets through trimming personnel resources.

You must step-up your game in order to succeed. No one is invincible from these cuts. High-level supervisors, whole departments, and especially those that do not excel at the office politics game and performance are all vulnerable.

Take my friend Chyou for example.

*Chyou's Story*

Chyou, an engineer in a firm of 2,000+, decided to ask for a change in her work-hours when she had her first child. The company touted that they were a "family business," but when hard times came and a downturn in the economy occurred, Chyou still wanted to maintain her focus on her family. At the same time, Chyou didn't focus on the core competencies she had and began to ignore the politically charged environment around her in the office. Chyou continued down this path of ignoring the outside world and would take every opportunity during the day that required socialization to throw-in a comment about focusing on her family.

While other people in the office would stay late, take the boss to lunch and stepped-up their game with regard to the political game, Chyou sat in her office and worked hard, never remembering to leave her office occasionally and work on her image with the office. After a few months, she had been routed from her high-standing in her boss's eyes and he asked her to leave during the second round of layoffs. Chyou could have saved her position if only she had paid attention to the changing environment around her. Her lack of attention to office politics lost her a job, and perhaps her career because it will be very difficult for her to get another position during these economically difficult times. And having followed-up with Chyou, I have since discovered that she has lost some of her self-worth and is now having difficulties in her home life. If only she had paid attention to the political needs in her office, perhaps she could have saved herself a lot of heartache.

*He who will not economize will have to agonize.*

*~ Confucius*

Illustration 27

Chyou's inability to change in the economically distressed times made her vulnerable and she failed to survive the concrete jungle. This is very similar to the animal's need to be successful during times of environmental difficulty such as drought or famine. Animals store food for the winter or build-up fat to sustain them through hibernation. Animals change their watering-holes if their normal one dries-out. Animals change with the season and the changes around them. And they will move to a greener pasture if the pasturage is lacking – or simply if that is part of their nomadic style.

Our survival in the corporate environment is the same. If you become stagnant and refuse to acknowledge the political game around you, your likelihood of success just dropped to near nothing. This is becoming more and more true as the economic situation becomes more grim. The corporate environment is ever-changing and you must keep raising the bar to succeed. And do not believe that you can escape the office politics jungle – no one escapes, and if you refuse to play, you get played out and will be eaten alive!

## **What makes you think you can escape the office politics jungle?!**

Many executives naively think that they can remain apolitical and still survive. This may have been the case several years ago when our grandfathers were CEO's and jobs were secure, but that is simply not the case now. Each generation since the 1960's has pushed the boundaries further and further until we look at the workforce now and see a very different face with very different goals than previous years. And as each new generation enters the workforce, we see more and more how abstaining from playing office politics can really affect a career.

That is not to say that this push is coming just from the young workers in the world, because it is a stream of thought from the marketplace and the tightening economy that is causing this shift toward office politics, too. Because each industry within each country and each economy of each country is intertwined with its twins in other countries, we are seeing entire shifts in thinking not just across a business or a firm, but across our entire civilization. This paradigm shift has affected each of us in a personal way that you may or may not recognize.

For example, have you ever shopped on the internet because it was convenient? Have you ever eaten at a fast-food restaurant because it was convenient? Have you ever hired someone to do something that you could do, but you just didn't want to (like cleaning your house, doing your laundry or walking your dog)? If you answered yes to any of these questions, you are part of a movement toward a more-convenient lifestyle, quite contrary to the lifestyles of old.

Just think about those same questions and how your grandfathers or even fathers would have answered when they were at the same place you are in your career. I know that my father would have answered: What's the internet? Fast-food, yuk! and No! He didn't do things for their convenience. Why, that would have been contrary to the "right" way to do things in his way of thinking.

*Convenience has become a way of life. Although one would never vacuum, walk the dog and dress for work – if it was physically possible and saved time, you might...*
*Illustration 5*

The main reason why office politics is intensifying is not clear – it is certainly due to many factors, but some that come to mind on the forefront leading the change include the rapid changes in the companies around us in response to the shorter and shorter boom and bust cycles. As a result, there is little or no job security left in the market for the majority of people. In order to survive, one needs to make a positive impression quickly. No one will know how you perform if you do not immediately take the opportunity and exhibit your own personal strengths. By stepping-up and being an advocate for your career you take with you the chance that no one will ever know the impact you can make in your business. And because bosses are human, carrying-on with their own lives, they are too busy to realize your worth over the long-term if you do not make it known. Additionally, younger executives are ambitious, stepping over those that may not move as quickly because they want to rise up as fast as possible. You must compete with them all in this office-jungle of the new-age.

The workplace has evolved and as a result, we need to change with it – or be played out during this most recent economic downturn.

The office has become a complex ecosystem rife with politics which must be navigated on a daily basis. If you believe that you aren't affected by them, you're just plain wrong. And if you believe that you can survive (much less thrive) without playing them (and playing them well), you're also just plain wrong. Everyone is affected and everyone is responsible for themselves. You must wake-up and realize – you must play office politics.

*If you don't play the office politics game, you will be eaten – alive!*
Illustration 6

If you do not play office politics, you will be eaten alive. There is no other way to view it. The office world today is too intricate of a machine to not see that it is fueled by office politics.

And though you might decide to ignore office politics, it will not ignore you. You must be an advocate for your career and do what you must if you want to survive. If you now stay out of office politics, step back and take a look at yourself and be honest. Ask yourself these questions:

1. Is your position stable?
2. Are you respected within your firm?
3. Does your leadership ask for your opinion before taking action?
4. Are you upwardly mobile?
5. Do you work well within a team?

If you can truthfully answer all of these questions affirmatively, you can feel free to throw this book in the trash (although there may be some valuable lessons for even you in this book). But if you answered negatively to even one of these questions, you are not playing the office politics game well – and ignoring it for any longer may get you played out.

So, how do you dig yourself out of the situation you've gotten yourself into? It may not be very easy given how long you've either avoided playing the game or how poorly you've been playing. Taking the lessons of this book, and perhaps picking up a few others may give you some tips for being more successful, but by no means is there a perfect book for your situation. You must learn how to build an arsenal of tools from which you can pull ideas on a continual basis. Only then can you know that you are playing at the best of your abilities.

And if the situation changes, don't panic. There will be many changes throughout your career. If you panic at the dawning of each, you will spend much of your life having anxiety and will never learn how to be calm and sure of yourself. So, read-on and learn how to attack change and how to prepare yourself for the possibilities that lie ahead. Take a message from what the animals can teach us and learn to play the game of office politics.

If you need a little push to decide that playing the game can be better than ignoring its existence, listen to the story my friend Aran had to tell.

*Aran's Story*

Aran came to work every day and left everyday on time. He did what he was asked to do and was more than happy to interact with someone if they instigated it. But his actions were very focused on getting the job done, and not interacting with those people in the office. Although he was pleasant to work with, he definitely didn't play to the office politics. Aran was well known to be a hard worker and managed his projects well, but those people that worked for him were not recognized, he wasn't recognized and when he got passed-over for an important promotion, the realization came to him – he was just not playing office politics, and had therefore missed-out!

Aran was furious with himself. He was smart, how did he miss this crucial lesson? So, he decided to take a new approach. Over the next few months, he watched what his more-successful counterparts did and how they behaved. He picked those activities that he preferred and liked what they did, and mirrored them. He singled-out those behaviors that they did that he disliked and he removed them from his own playlist.

The change was slow, but it was evident to Aran that the perception in the office toward him was changing. The people that worked on his team were working harder for him because he was freer with praise. The other team-leaders that he worked with asked him for his opinion more often. And when an executive level meeting was called at the end of the year, Aran was invited! Aran was thrilled to see that truly there had been changes in his behavior that had effected change in his status within the office. Following the big meeting with the executives, Aran was promoted to their number. "We had wanted to do this for a while," he was told, "You seemed to have potential, but something was just holding us back." Aran knew that what had been holding them back had now changed and he was now a truly successful player of the office political game.

Aran's lesson is that you can change your perception within the office. You can motivate others to rely on your judgment, you can change their view of you, and you can promote yourself through playing the game well. Now, there are no guarantees in life and surely, even if we play office politics, there can still be that occasional hiccup which lands us in a sticky situation. But if we acknowledge that there are only nebulous defeats and indefinable victories, we can accept them all as victories in learning a lesson in how to do it better the next time. However, it is up to you to apply the lessons and play the game. And because you are competing with each and every one of your co-workers, you are your own responsibility, and must be an advocate for your own career.

And your advocacy for your career must infuse every part of your work-day. You must focus not on the immediate alone, but also the greater picture – but don't forget the immediate situation while you focus on the future. Each year, each week, each day, each hour and each interaction requires all of the attention and focus you can provide it in order for you to succeed.

## **Influences of Office Politics in Person-to-Person Interaction**

While you must focus on all of the goals within your career, you must start with each interaction, as they will be the building blocks for the rest of your career goals. And there may be many interactions throughout a day, much less a week or year that you might encounter – as many as there are people within your office!

Just as there are many people who work together in your corporation, the jungle is full of animals of a wide variety. A look at our interactions and the similarity of animal interactions can really illustrate how similar we are to our animal friends. And by viewing how similar we are, we can look to the animals to reveal how our innate instincts might be of use in day-to-day interactions.

We can break-down our interactions (and our animal brethrens' interactions) into three categories: Confrontational, Friendly, and Routine. By taking a look at each of these three interaction types and how some animal friends react similarly to the human species, we can see how helpful taking ideas from the animal world might be.

Confrontational interactions can be described best by a quick synopsis from the corporate jungle:

> Two co-workers, vying for the same promotion, must compete for their bosses' accolades to secure the desirable position. Although the fight is not as bloody in visual terms, the fight can be terribly vicious, and the outcome just as uncertain. One co-worker may tell the boss how poorly the other guy performed on a task, while the other co-worker does the same. In a situation like that, no one can win.

We are finding that as the economy begins to falter and resources such as jobs and funding become more and more scarce, these situations are coming up far more frequently. This is no surprise as animals will often turn to violence as well when resources get scarce.

Let's take the same two co-workers, turn them into gazelles and see how the interaction changes by moving from the corporate jungle to the real jungle.

Two male gazelles find that they both lust after the same particularly attractive young-lady gazelle. The fight is on! The older, more seasoned gazelle fights the younger, more virile gazelle. Ultimately, one will win, however, the confrontation can be both bloody and the outcome uncertain. Often, both combatants may come away with mortal wounds, or wounds which make them too vulnerable to a predatory attack.

*Fighting over a lady and fighting over resources are the same thing!*
Illustration 7

Now, let's step back and see what might have happened to avert this disastrous situation. Certainly, most of the time, gazelles will never come to full blows. If they come close, it's in marking territory or in taking stances in front of one another. Sometimes, office battles can be won in the same manner. It may be all about posturing and making the scene right for you to ensure a battle-victory. Consider taking the high-road and not complaining in order to get a higher-victory – not looking like a whiner to your boss!

The friendly interaction takes on a very different tone in the concrete jungle. One example of this type of interaction would be:

> One project manager has won a bid for a big project which is far too man-hour intensive for his team to complete within the given schedule. So, she approaches her colleague, another project manager with too little to keep his team profitable for the short period of time which, conveniently, the big project is due. The two project managers broker a deal – she'll give his team some additional work from the big project, keeping them profitable, and he in return will provide her with the personnel to complete the project on time.

These types of interactions may become fewer as the economy begins to worsen. It is my advice that you take every opportunity to enjoy and make the most of friendly interactions you might have in this recession era.

Similarly, the real jungle has friendly interactions. For example, if our two executives are now department heads of different types of groups – a den of lions and a pack of hyenas, the interaction would go something like this:

While wandering the jungle, the hyena comes upon a kill that the lion recently took down – and that the lion is still eating. Although the lion and the hyena are both predators and both salivate over the thought of the warm gazelle steak at their feet, the hyena backs-off. The hyena will wait patiently, biding its time, until the lion has had his fill. When the lion is done and has left the scene, the hyena will eat his fill, too.

*The hyena can get what he wants if he sits patiently and waits to have dinner after the lion has his.*
Illustration 8

This interaction may not seem overly friendly, but indeed it is about as friendly as one can get in the jungle. Certainly, it is this type of partnership that has kept the hyena alive for many years – they are scavengers first, then hunters. And the relationship is good, too for the lion, because the presence of the hyena keeps other scavengers from bothering the lion. In a way, the hyena guards the lion's back while the lion eats – although from the hyena's perspective, he is just protecting his meal until the lion is done!

The office can be viewed in the same manner – although you may not see the advantage in sharing work or in helping another team, there is always advantage to be had in getting someone's favor for a future use!

The final, and most frequent of interactions are known as routine interactions. The routine is not just the "every-day" but also those interactions where there is no attack and no friendly behavior. In the office environment, the following would be an example of this type of behavior:

> When two executives of equal authority, with no previous history of positive or negative interaction find themselves in the same conference room, they acknowledge one another and behave in a congenial manner. They may nod to each other or discuss a topic, but the interaction is simply congenial. At the end of the meeting, neither of the executives will walk away with a new friend or enemy, if there is no confrontation.

As the economy continues its downward spiral, we may find that these types of situations become more stressed and begin to turn into more confrontational than routine. It will be your responsibility as a participant in these types of interactions to maintain a cool head and behave rationally.

Our animal brethren also have routine interactions in which neither animal is required to react in any way save congeniality. A good example would be the interaction between the elephant and the hippopotamus.

> The elephant herd goes to the watering-hole to get a drink. There, a hippopotamus is playing in the water. Although they both acknowledge the other's presence, they do nothing. They have no need to fight as they share resources such as the watering hole well and they have no reason to react positively to one another. When done, the elephant leaves and the hippopotamus changes nothing, as long as no confrontation occurs.

It is highly unlikely that confrontation would occur in either this office situation or this jungle situation. In both, there is no reason for a fight or reason to be friends. If there is no favor to be won, and no fight to be fought, then the interaction is just routine.

*When to be defensive and when to take the offense*

By taking a look at how similarly animals and people react in their respective jungles, we can take a cue from the animals if we are trying to remember our own animal instincts regarding interactions with each other. And it is these animal interactions that we're trying to remember – just those things that we have innately within ourselves, but that are hiding deep inside.

Although there are three types of interactions, each type can only be approached in two different manners: Defensive and Offensive.

Defensive mechanisms are used when someone is looking to attack you, which, if you are like me, you assume this is likely to be the case all the time. A good defense can keep you from being in an offensive position later. But offensive mechanisms have their place, too. The offensive stances can carry you through a battle and ensure that you survive. Since each has its place in the concrete jungle, we'll explore both and their appropriate uses.

Let's look at the most popular methods of defensive maneuvering: Strong Work Ethic, Working in a Team, and Avoiding Confrontation.

*Strong Work Ethic*

A strong work ethic is the basis for success, take our friends the beavers for example. The beaver works hard all year long to build a little den in which to raise his young. But because he works so hard, his "little den" blocks rivers and becomes dams which can change the entire ecosystem of the water body. Imagine any other animal (besides the human with a bull-dozer) that can effect such massive change. If you can re-route a river without a bull-dozer, give it a shot, but the beavers do it every day.

This strong work ethic pays-off for the beaver. Not only do they get a nice place to raise the baby-beavers that has a lake-side view, they also have a warm place with clean drinking water and easy fish to catch. It's all a fantastic dream, and all because the beaver insists on working hard to build and maintain his little dam.

*Hard work pays-off for the beaver.*
*Illustration 9*

*Working in a Team*

There is security in numbers, working with a team is always better, as the monkeys easily illustrate. The monkey, be it chimpanzee, gorilla, or spider monkey always works in a team to find food, shelter or to protect themselves from enemies. This is key, since the individual monkey is easy prey for many a predator, has a hard time finding adequate amounts of food and may or may not be able to find good shelter. This safety in numbers method becomes extremely clear when we look to the social grooming nature of the monkey. All monkeys are fairly well known for grooming one another. This keeps ticks and other disease-carrying pests from invading each monkey's personal space, and these same bugs provide a source of protein for the groomer. If this type of behavior did not exist, monkeys would be a population of diseased animals as opposed to one of the most successful species on the planet.

*By working in teams, the monkeys are a much more successful species.*
Illustration 10

*Avoiding Confrontation*

The last popular defensive maneuver is avoiding unnecessary confrontation. Often, in the jungle, this is accomplished by simply waiting until the time is right. Look at our friend the hyena that we talked about previously, he waited until the time was right to get the food the lion so conveniently left behind – and he didn't even really have to work for it! By avoiding the potential confrontation, the hyena not only avoided the injury he surely would have received from the fight the lion would give him, but he also was able to eat in relative peace, knowing that the nearby lion and his den were satiated. Unfortunately, the hyena does have to compete with other hyenas and other scavengers. However, since he knows that to be patient and wait will produce a good result (his full stomach), he will often avoid confrontation with the lion, a fight he will surely lose.

In the concrete jungle, our defensive attitudes can often turn out better than confrontation might have. My friend Mitsuho learned this lesson.

<u>Mitsuho's Story</u>

Mitsuho worked hard, taking every opportunity to increase his department's productivity by increasing efficiency and effectiveness. He would stay late to ensure that a deliverable would make it to the client by the due date. And he integrated himself into a team of like-minded department leaders, asking them for advice and sharing his own regarding similar projects and tasks. Then, one day, one of his co-workers, a guy a few years older than him and with far more skills at the office politicking game, slighted Mitsuho.

The older department head made a comment to a client which lost Mitsuho a project. Mitsuho could have gotten angry and made their shared supervisor aware of the slight against him. But Mitsuho did not. And, to Mitsuho's surprise, the other gentleman realized his mistake and worked to make amends. The other gentleman even approached their supervisor, explained what he had done and asked that the supervisor not punish Mitsuho for losing the project. In the end, Mitsuho came out of the situation looking like the hero, simply because he took a defensive approach to his leadership.

But if you do choose to be defensive by refusing to interact – beware. You may become the reluctant tortoise, always hiding in his shell. In Mitsuho's situation, rather than being too reticent and overly-defensive, he balanced his defensive tactics. Had he taken the offensive tactic, he may not have left the situation looking so good.

Offensive tactics should only be used when confrontation is the only way to solve the issue. However, sometimes, confrontation is the only way. This decision may come to you in many forms which might even include protecting your employees and young professionals who may or may not know better how best to protect themselves. This is similar to the aggressive stance that the lioness takes when her cubs are threatened. If cubs were left on their own other beasts may find that they are a tasty snack. But, they could also become a tasty snack to males which stumble upon the den. If the lioness doesn't aggressively protect her cubs (sometimes to the point of death), then the cubs become lunch!

***Regard your soldiers as your children, and they will follow you into the deepest valleys. Look on them as your own beloved sons, and they will stand by you even unto death!***
***~ Sun Tzu, the Art of War***

Illustration 27

Attacking a problem head-on is another offensive tactic that is very popular in both the animal-jungle and the concrete jungle. The shark is an excellent example. The shark is always in search of a meal – because they have a particular problem: they require a great deal of food to keep their bodies going. So, to solve this problem, they spend hours hunting and attacking their prey. And every prey gets the same respect, they are all attacked head-on. The shark does not stalk a prey for days, run the prey down or hide in waiting until prey passes its cave, the shark attacks, eats and leaves.

*The shark attacks all his meals an problems head-on. He is known fo this tactic and achieves respect.*
*Illustration 11*

This type of tactic is crucial for the concrete jungle. Attacking problems head-on is sometimes the only way to solve them. Often, people will ignore a problem or try to satisfy the immediate need without looking to the long-term need. This kind of tactic may be appropriate for short-term issues, however, to attack a problem head-on is the only sure way to resolve long-term difficulties. The current financial crisis and resulting crash of the world economy has direct relationship to ignoring problems and not attacking them head-on when they first present themselves. Surely, if the immediate reaction to the crash had been an increase in the regulation of the financial world, we could have avoided many of the problems we are currently seeing.

The final offensive tactic which is used most frequently is taking advantage of an opportunity when presented, even if it might appear to be distasteful at the time.

Vultures are an animal with a distasteful image and a distasteful approach to their offensive tactics. The modern concept of the vulture is as a nasty carrion eater which searches alone in a desert for its meals. But as stated in the first chapter, every animal has a place in the ecosystem. The vulture and, similarly, other animals which prey on the dead, have a critical role to play. Their feeding on the animals which have died keeps diseases from spreading and cleans-up other predator's messes.

You may not want to be a vulture, but everyone sometimes is forced to do things that they may not like. Even non-aggressive animals may turn extremely aggressive if there is a lack of food. Animals are more vicious when fighting for their survival, and the same is true with human beings when they are fighting for job preservation. Even if you don't like taking advantage of a presented opportunity, it may be in your best interest to do so in order to survive, regardless of your personal feelings.

My friend Mingmei was put into a very difficult situation to learn when it really is necessary to be offensive. And her situation certainly was unsavory, and she felt like a vulture at the time, but she saved her career and learned that sometimes the difficult situation is one which you can transform into a positive experience.

*Mingmei's Story*

Mingmei was a Senior Project Manager within her corporation. Unfortunately, she and her boss did not communicate clearly during the execution of a very politically-charged assignment. Mingmei presented her findings to the City's review board and was crushed when they came back with a denial. Mingmei's boss then proceeded to tell the board of directors at her firm that it was Mingmei's fault that they had received a denial from the City. Mingmei was furious. *How could he say that when he is as much to blame as I?* She asked herself.

**He will win who knows when to fight and when not to fight.**

**~ *Sun Tzu, the Art of War***

Illustration 27

46

Mingmei stepped back and calmly determined that attacking this problem head-on was probably the best way to save her career and take the advantage that her boss had unwittingly given her. Although confronting the issue was going to be uncomfortable, Mingmei approached the Chief Executive Officer and asked for an audience. When they discussed the events, the CEO agreed with Mingmei that her boss was simply overreacting and the CEO even told Mingmei that he had previously had a suspicion that her boss was doing so even before Mingmei approached him. For putting all of the blame on Mingmei, her boss was summarily fired and Mingmei promoted in his place.

Mingmei faced many problems and chose to confront only those which she could control, playing to her strengths and acknowledging her weaknesses as well. However, one thing that Mingmei also did which ensured the positive outcome was being conscious of the state of her office. We'll explore this more in the next chapter, but to touch on Mingmei's situation, it is clear that she played not only to her own abilities, but also to the state of the office around her.

## **When the State of the Office Influences Action**

Mingmei recognized that the state of the office can strongly influence the politics of the office. And with the state of the economy faltering, it will become more and more important to be flexible in the face of chance based on the state of the office. Certainly if people are afraid for their jobs, many may resort to dirty tactics, even if they would not in a less-pressured environment. Animals react the same way. Many animals will easily and happily share resources, if they are plentiful. However, if resources are scarce, some animals have been known to eat even their own young, taking what they need in the face of scarce sources. This may be the current situation we are seeing with the economy. To resolve the current crisis, we may need to approach the economy as one would approach a corporate turnaround.

Corporate turnaround methodology can be broken-down into three simple phases: Surgery, Resuscitation, and Nursing.

> Surgery Phase: The organization needs to restructure itself to face the new harsh reality. This is for companies in intensive care units and financial control takes precedence
>
> Resuscitation Phase: The organization needs to re-vitalize its revenues and profits. This is for companies to grow its business and marketing takes precedence.
>
> Nursing Phase: The organization needs to build a corporate culture that is innovative, fast and flexible. This is for companies to grow and sustain that growth and human resource take precedence.

All three of which can also apply to office politics as the state of the office can greatly influence the actions of those around you – and which should also influence your reactions. Certainly if the firm you work for is in the Surgery stage of corporate turnaround, your outlook needs to transform to adapt to this situation. Or if your behavior is contrary to the current nature of the firm, you may be labeled as a pest. And as your firm slowly moves from the Surgery to Resuscitation and then Nursing phases, you must always be transforming with your environment, evolving as it evolves. You must change your political stance as your company goes through these three phases – in other words, one needs to understand the situation and behave accordingly, or act politically correct.

Animals shift and change dependent on their species' inherent strengths and weaknesses within a changing environment. And our environments are the same. Your political style may need to change according to the phases. Whereas a predatory style, such as that of the lion, shark, or crocodile may thrive in the Surgery phase where survival is critical, for the Resuscitation phase the social animals may do well such as the monkey, dogs. For the Nursing phase, certainly a more laid-back style would be more appropriate such as the eagle, the bear or the beaver. Whereas the chameleon may be able to modify its behavior enough to survive each phase without missing a beat.

*Phase 1: Surgery*

This phase is described in the corporate turnaround philosophy as being a more immediate and damage-containment method. This type of method would be described as a tactic for companies in the intensive care unit. While financial control and cash flow management are emphasized, an autocratic and transactional leadership style is required to make this type of company save itself from ruin.

The appropriate method of behavior for the employee will be different for each individual. However, in general terms, management which is trying to revive a firm will be relieved and excited to find an employee which is decisive and sure. Good examples to immolate if your firm is in this phase might be those predators which attack problems head-on and deliver hard-hitting tactics.

*Surgery in the jungle is absurd – but in the office may be necessary for a healthy firm.*
Illustration 12

These types of predators could be the lion, shark, or crocodile would be well suited for the Surgery phase of a corporation's lifecycle. Certainly the lion does not balk at attacking the gazelle for dinner, nor does the shark second-guess itself before taking a bite out of a seal. And the crocodile wouldn't dream of attacking a hippopotamus, but knows that the turtle will be a quick meal. Because the Surgery phase requires this type of surety of self and a focused intensity on financial controls, the same tactics must be used by employees seeking to take advantage of the state of the office.

*Kanya's Story*

For Kanya, every day was a new day and every problem was a new problem to be attacked with innovative and cutting-edge solutions. Now, she had been at three different firms before she realized that sometimes, people don't like it when you're too aggressive in putting forth your ideas. But Kanya couldn't help herself – if she saw a problem, she simply had to attempt a solution. She had landed in her fourth job since graduating from college and was still considered very young. She knew that this last firm was really taking a chance on hiring her – and that she was taking a chance on them, since the firm wasn't doing very well. There was a lot of talk about possibly closing the firm, until they were purchased by a competitor. Layoffs began and when a new CEO came into the picture, Kanya was very concerned that she might be next on the chopping block.

However, when Kanya got into a conference room with her CEO (on his second week on the job), she noticed something different about his approach to the business. So, when a problem was laid on the table by one of Kanya's co-workers for which Kanya had the perfect, but daring, idea for a solution – she simply offered it up for criticism. The room seemed timid to grasp onto her idea at first, but she was allowed to attempt this solution before the end of the meeting. So, as soon as she left the room, she got to work. First, she determined which resources she would need, then she executed the plan, keeping both her co-workers and her CEO well-informed throughout the process. Her plan worked and her new CEO was delighted!

Kanya's story is a good example of how being decisive can get you far, if you are in the right situation. However, Kanya's behavior at three other firms won her nothing but unhappiness and failure. It's key to note as well that she required heavy mentoring to continue to be successful at her new firm when it began to transition into the Resuscitation Phase. Kanya was no chameleon to be able to change her colors without a lot of help from those around her!

*Phase 2: Resuscitation*

This phase is best described by a company which needs to grow its sales revenue and come back stronger than before. The emphasis for a firm in this type of situation is on marketing and expanding its consumer base. A democratic and transactional leadership style with a bit of transformational leadership is the most successful combination for this phase of corporate resuscitation.

For this phase, management will be looking for those employees who can build strong networks and bring value to the firm by increasing efficiency or easily pleasing consumers. This requires a social person, easy-going with a focus on personal interactions. Animals which might provide a good model for people in this situation might be the monkey because of its social nature or the dog due to its loyalty.

Of all the social animals I think of the monkey because of their strong tendency to touch each other and the dog because of their tendency to play together. The monkey can spend up to eight hours a day grooming each other (thank you National Geographic for that statistic). Wow! That's a lot of time to be spending picking little bugs and dirt out of someone else's fur.

Dogs on the other hand spend a lot of their time when they're together playing and rolling together. I have two and they are always tugging on toys together and chasing each other around the house. And both of these animals are very loyal to whomever they consider to be their family, be it the other monkeys in their group or the people that they live with. In the Resuscitation Phase, these attributes are highly desirable because they can work well with others and can be great customer-servers.

*Bae's Story*

Bae is a strong believer in the "fun at work" philosophy. He's at the top of the list when anyone organizes a company picnic or friendly game. He's also continually working with his customers to make sure that he spends quality time with them in a social setting, getting to know them as more than just a customer. This came in very handy when he came to a firm which had recently progressed out of the Surgery Phase. Bae was working as he normally does to build a strong client base. He was spending time with his clients and spending time with his new co-workers when they were doing social activities.

But Bae didn't feel like others in the organization were doing as well with these social aspects, so he started mentoring those young professionals that were interested in his success. Bae was quickly singled-out by his Executive Vice President as a strong leader – simply because he had taken under-wing several young professionals and tutored them in some of the more social aspects of network building. His Executive Vice President appreciated his efforts and implored other managers to follow Bae's style.

*Phase 3: Nursing*

This phase puts a strong emphasis on building a strong corporate culture that promotes flexibility, speed and innovativeness. The focus is on human resource, the leadership style is spiritual, empowering, building a veritable corporate immune system to fight diseases. This phase is based solidly on building this immune system as a means of preventive medicine through a natural and holistic approach.


Those employees who will thrive in this environment will be those with a conciliatory nature, happy to solve problems through compromise and understanding. This type of person has to be hard-working though, making an impact in the realm of business development while working on a winning strategy for the future. Animals which might be positive role-models for the people in this phase should be focused on looking to the future and hard-working.

The eagle, one of the most majestic birds has a reputation for its speed and agility when attacking prey. There are many animals which have these same qualities, but because the eagle also chooses one mate with which to stay with for the remainder of its life, I put it in a different category of long-term thinkers. This makes the eagle a very good example for the Nursing Phase because it meets and exceeds the attributes most likely to succeed in this phase. The bear is also a long-term thinker in my opinion because of the enormous stores it must create to survive a winter of hibernation. And the beaver, too is a good example for the hard work it exhibits throughout its lifetime of creating dams.

These same types of people will be successful in the concrete jungle when their firm is in the Nursing Phase. For example, my friend Channary. It isn't hard to believe Channary's story ended-up on the Nursing Phase. Having known her in her personal life, one would have imagined that her conciliatory nature in her corporate persona would win her this phase easily. But she also has a wonderful knack for solving problems through a holistic approach as opposed to solving only one piece of an issue. Her innovative and inspiring nature is also what set her apart from all of my other acquaintances as the prime example for the Nursing Phase.

*Channary's Story*

Always a negotiator, Channary took to her new job with a firm in its Nursing Phase with alacrity. She was hired to be the Director of Research and Development, but knew she would need to also be a facilitator for other groups in order to get their input on her projects. Channary always seemed to find a way to solve conflict in her old firm through understanding and compromise, but being a facilitator of such negotiations was going to be a new job for her. However, she felt she was up to the task. Until she met Raj.

Raj was the head of the Marketing department. Channary thought that he would be her greatest ally in getting products from her department to the customer – but she couldn't have been more wrong. Raj was angry at the world and unhappy about being put over a department that he felt was useless. And his behavior really did just that – made the department useless.

Channary's job was truly hampered by Raj's dislike of his own position. Channary was concerned that she would fail because Raj wanted to be unsuccessful. But she would try anyway. So, she set out to win Raj over on her first "sell" job to him. She set-up a test group, got the results, obtained all of the in-house testing results and set-up her meeting with Raj. She went in with a strong message of working together to get this probable consumer product off the ground. She sold the project to Raj as if she were selling a refrigerator to a man in Siberia!

But then Raj started throwing up red flags. He didn't think the product would work – and he thought that the backlash on the company would do more harm than the good that would come from launching the product. He espoused the "rifle" method of marketing products as opposed to the "shotgun" method that he accused Channary of espousing, since she wanted to sell "every" product they invented in R&D.

Channary felt ashamed that Raj would assume that of her. And so she told him. But she also told him that she understood where he was coming from and why he might feel this way – why they had not really even interacted in the few months since she had been at the firm. So, she told him that she would go back to the drawing-board and take some of his advice and bring him a better product which he could sell.

By saying those things to Raj, his understanding of her position dawned on him. He apologized for being so rude and said that he would go ahead and take the specs from her for this product and see "what he could do." The next time Channary came in with a new idea, Raj was much more excited to accept her proposal without argument – and Channary found out that Raj had sold no less than 500,000 of the first product she had presented to him!

Winning over Raj had been the only thing that had held the last R&D Director back from being a success in the firm. And the Principal in Charge took notice very quickly that Channary and Raj seemed to have a good working relationship. As a result, he passed along praise to his boss and Channary and Raj both received very nice bonuses for the work on their first project! But all of that one-time success aside, Channary had taken the time to build a partnership with Raj, something no one else in her position before her had done. And because of this investment she will have a much longer-term success with this firm than others had before her.

So, as we can see, there are some personality types that can thrive very well within a given situation. However, I am not trying to say that only one type of person with one personality type can win in each phase. You can easily look to the chameleon for their approach to changing their colors based on the situation at hand. Surely if the chameleon, a tiny little lizard, can change himself to succeed in his environment, we humans can do so with little or no issue. We should simply analyze our situation and determine the best solution for the present. We should each stay on guard and be aware that to avoid change is to go the way of the dinosaurs and become extinct.

*The chameleon can hide on the leaf and save himself from the predator by being flexible in his outward appearance and stealthy in his actions.*
*Illustration 13*

The chameleon is no fighter, so perhaps even he would not win in every situation, but rather blend-in with the crowd, taking on their characteristics until the situation changed again. However, this is no way to become the king of the office-jungle. The lion is not a chameleon, the shark is also no lizard. So, how do we ensure that we can succeed? What would the animals tell us to help us succeed? And how can we superimpose what we can learn from the animal world to our own tips for success?

## Five Ways to Succeed

## Becoming King of the Jungle

Standing out from the herd is critical if you want to lead – and is becoming more critical for simple survival in the economically distressed environment. In the jungle, the leader of the pack is chosen through feats of strength and posturing. In the office environment, battles are won in the same way.

Feats of strength are won or lost in an office dependent on your position, tenure, the trust your partners have in you, and many other factors that are generally built-up through years of playing the office politics game well. Simply put, this is because although in the jungle the animals can literally test each other – in the office, we simply cannot arm-wrestle every day to see who's the strongest (although it might be fun).

*Arm-wrestling would be silly in the office, but we do find other ways to exhibit our strength during confrontations.*
Illustration 14

Posturing starts with carrying yourself with an air of leadership and thoughtfulness. And it's best if these characteristics are portrayed voluntarily and throughout your interactions with people. Assuming the mantle of authority by acknowledging others, teaching when the opportunity arises, and leading, without being asked are the easiest and most gratifying ways to be recognized. Truly, when supervisors and co-workers look around the office for someone to be promoted or to lead important efforts, if you have consistently and voluntarily lead for some time, the choice will be obvious.

*If you would take, you must first give, this is the beginning of intelligence.*
*~ Lao Tzu*

Illustration 27

My friend Yeshe could write an entire book about assuming the mantle of leadership and authority. He was born knowing how to behave as a leader – even before he really was.

### <u>Yeshe's Story</u>

Yeshe started at the firm as a part of a team of other young professionals just like him. He was concerned that he was going to be lost in the crowd and he desperately desired to be a leader. At the same time, those that he had started working at the firm were close to him and he valued their close teamwork. So, instead of taking a cut-throat approach, he decided to be supportive of his co-workers, helping them to succeed and hoping that it would help him succeed, too.

Now, this was a great tactic. Yeshe's supervisors saw immediately how helpful he was teaching the other young professionals what he knew and sharing his expertise. Also, Yeshe's boss noticed that Yeshe always thanked his co-workers for a job well-done and that Yeshe would tell others freely if another co-worker had worked late to finish a project or done other accolade-worthy act. By promoting his co-workers through praise and taking the opportunity to teach, his supervisors took notice and promoted Yeshe at the earliest opportunity. Yeshe continued to grow by growing his teammates and has gained many personal rewards as a result.

*Respect yourself and others will respect you.*

*~ Confucius*

Illustration 27

The lion is the perfect animal-kingdom example to illustrate becoming king of the jungle – because he is the king of the jungle! The lion does occasionally play at exhibiting his strength through wrestling and aggressively defending his territory – don't think that I do not acknowledge this fact. However, much of his standing with the pack and much of why he only occasionally has to express his strength is posturing. The lion will spend much time marking his territory, sounding that deep-throated frightening roar and making that mane grow to astonishing size. By exhibiting these strong features and illustrating for the world to see that he is king, the lion convinces the den to let him lead, allowing him to choose when they will hunt, where they will hunt, and allowing him to be the only male to mate with the females of the den.

*The lion will mark his territory as a dog would – and we do the same in the office!*
Illustration 15

So, what is the lion's first secret – presentation. We've all heard the saying "presentation is 99% of the work." Well, the saying is right. Many times, in the animal world, presentation is what it takes to convince another animal of strength or health, convincing the supposedly weaker to leave the resources to you. This is the same for humans – sometimes presentation is all it takes to convince someone you're the best and should therefore get the praise. Take Yamuna, for example:

*Yamuna's Story*

Yamuna was a project manager with a flair for the way things look and the way her team looked was no exception. She increased the level of quality of her team's work by ensuring that the end product was well put-together and professional in appearance. Yamuna relied on her team to ensure that there was technical reliability in their product, and she focused on the value she could bring by making the end product "pretty."

By adding a little flair or "sexiness" to the exhibits and making sure that each document appeared as professional as it could possibly be, Yamuna was able to bring the level of quality to a new high in her firm. And Yamuna didn't stop there. She made sure that her team members dressed professionally and presented her clients with a product that was always top-notch. This made Yamuna stand out to her supervisors and to the firm's top leaders. As a result, she was invited to join their ranks a full five years before any other executive had been invited to the same.

If the lion isn't a good enough example to illustrate that presentation is key, look at the peacock. The male peacock is not a large bird, something smaller than a turkey, even. But predators run from him and female peacocks flock to him – all for those silly, obscenely large and unwieldy feathers sticking out from his backside!

Predators run from the peacock because his tail feathers have the oddly familiar looking dark spots at the top which would appear to any good carnivore as eyes – which would make the peacock much larger than the true bird. And the girls, well they flock to the guy peacocks for the same reason – those obnoxious feathers protect the males, making them that much more desirable to the females!

*The peacock has great presentation which keeps him from being a predator's meal and gets him the ladies!*
Illustration 16

The second most important tactic that the lion illustrates is that teaming-up is critical – and that never throwing his den-mates under the bus is a large part of that. The lion will make certain that each and every one of his den-mates have eaten before he stops hunting for the day – he needs his team to survive. Our offices are no different. We are dependent on one another for survival and must cultivate those relationships to ensure our individual success. Tamayo learned that lesson well:

*Tamayo's Story*

Tamayo worked for many years on a one-person project. Tamayo had never had to work with anyone except for her boss. But when her boss was transferred away, Tamayo was placed in a team with many people. At first, she was leery of the other people, thinking that they might be out to get her, but as time went on, Tamayo began to learn how to easily work with her team. Then, one night, Tamayo discovered a mistake on a set of plans that one of her co-workers had made. It was late and the project was due the next day.

So, Tamayo politely approached her co-worker. *There is a mistake,* she said, but she didn't stop there, *But I think I have a solution, if you have time to stick around tonight with me to work it out.* Tamayo's co-worker was so relieved that Tamayo hadn't been upset or made a big deal out of the mistake that he was more than happy to help resolve the issue with her that night. Then, in the morning, the co-worker took the finished product to their boss and told her all about how Tamayo had saved them! Tamayo's boss then called her to discuss the situation and praised Tamayo for her teamwork and quick-thinking. And then, he mentioned how Tamayo might have reacted in a negative manner – and the quick displeasure that he would have shown if she had. Tamayo was so relieved that she had avoided that major misstep!

The wolf behaves in a similar fashion. The wolf is beneficent, sharing food, playing games, and rotating the responsibility of chores with his brothers. The wolves will attack the prey as a team, leaving behind those in the den to tend the young if necessary. When the killing is done, the wolves share-out the meal, taking back plenty for the "babysitter" den mates to eat and share to the pups. When not hunting, they all guard the den closely, males, females, old, young and every type in-between sharing in the responsibility and the fun of playing together. Often, their playing replaces the aggression that might be seen in other types of animals, allowing them to test each other's strengths in a more gentle setting.

The final lesson from the king of the jungle is: Making shrewd and wise decisions based on knowledge can never harm your standing in the jungle! I had a boss once that understood this philosophy well and used it to his advantage. Here is a story from his very successful career:

*Dian's Story*

Dian got a call on a Friday afternoon from his best client. This client was a national client with a knack for bringing very lucrative projects to Dian. And this Friday was no exception. However, the project had to be complete by Tuesday afternoon and would require that the team work through the weekend and perhaps very late nights to accomplish it. The client was very gracious when Dian told them that he needed a few minutes to make the decision regarding whether or not to take on the task.

As Dian hung-up the phone, he started thinking about all the things that his team would need if they were going to accomplish the project. He also started thinking about one of his team members whose wife had a new baby and needed to be home with her. Dian listed out what they would need for the weekend and the schedule that would need to be followed. He made sure that there would be enough people to accomplish the task, then, when he had a good plan in place, he called his team together. Dian presented his work plan to the team, putting an emphasis on getting the client to pay for meals, overtime, and special bonuses for each team member.

Dian asked each of the team to vote on whether or not to take on this task, and he was well rewarded for his efforts – they each voted "yes." When Dian called the client back, they were so excited that Dian agreed to do the work, they were happy to pay for the extra items Dian had determined he needed. Simply because he sat down and worked out exactly what it would take to do the task and had made an effort to ensure that everyone on his team had buy-in, Dian won the biggest project he had ever had.

Though the lion does provide us with a good example of making wise and true decisions, the fox embodies the concept. A fox will watch a chicken-roost for days if necessary to make certain that it knows when the danger is least for it to attack. When the fox determines that the danger is least, he will sneak into the roost, taking only what he needs to sustain himself. But the best part is, he will come back! Because he is wise to a safe and easily accessible hen-house and already knows the patterns, the fox can raid for a long while – avoiding capture almost every time!

But even the wily fox cannot avoid capture every time – and to believe that would put you at folly. So, how does the fox avoid believing himself un-catchable? Easy, he doesn't buy into the myth that he is capable of avoiding capture every time. He acknowledges that he must remain stealthy and creep away unseen – or face failure and certain death.

## Five Ways to Fail

## What the animals can tell us to avoid

Just as the fox must avoid buying-into the myth that he is un-catchable, there are many myths about office politics which can lead us to failure if we blindly follow them. And this is becoming more and more evident during this economically stressed time. If we cannot think beyond these old myths and learn to be flexible with the changing times, we are doomed to failure. So, what are these myths and how do we avoid them?

If you try, surely you can think of some that may apply to your own career. In my observations, there are five sure pitfalls that almost every one of us humans runs into throughout the course of our career:

*"If I just 'toe the party line' and stay loyal to my boss, I can't fail."*

*"I'm indispensable. They can't find fault with me!"*

*"I work hard – that's good enough."*

*"My boss loves me. Who cares if the other people in the office like me?!"*

*"If I mind my own business, no one will bother me."*

Each of these dangerous attitudes can be assumed without you even knowing. They can be unconscious attitudes that grow from the tiny seed of being proud of one's accomplishments. But by taking a stance to monitor your attitudes and by looking to the potential for disaster, you can avoid even a hint of these undesirable stances. By looking at the way animals fail or flourish with these same attitudes, we might be able to make better decisions for long-term success.

*"If I just 'toe the party line' and stay loyal to my boss, I can't fail."*


The myth that loyalty is all that you need to succeed has been debunked repeatedly in recent years. I have personally seen where many have failed because they assumed that the loyalty and devotion they have provided their supervisor or mentor is enough to carry them to success. If all you can see yourself doing is following the same person for the rest of your career, riding on the coattails of the ones before you, you're in trouble. This is a road to failure in so many instances.

Jay is an example of the disastrous consequences that can come from being overly-loyal.

### *Jay's Story*

Jay was a Junior Practice Builder in a large firm. He had worked with the same Senior Practice Builder for many years, but after a small project had financial problems which were partly to blame on both Jay and his Senior Practice Builder, Jay found himself the scapegoat. But Jay refused to speak out against his Senior Practice Builder because they were "friends." Shortly after the costly budget overruns on the project were blamed on Jay, he was asked to resign. Although Jay was able to find another position at a different firm within a few weeks, still the loss of wages affected his personal life and he took a large hit to his self-worth.

Clearly loyalty is not enough to sustain a career, and this is often also the case within the animal world. A faithful and loyal old wolf is still an old wolf in the eyes of the pack. When he is no longer useful and can no longer sustain himself, he will leave the pack and find a place to die. The same goes for many other animals – even domesticated cats and dogs. Most animals will either acknowledge that they are no longer contributing to the pack and leave, or if they are too saddled to know, then they are simply ushered out of the heard and left to die. Even bison will push the older, lamer members of the herd to the edges, sacrificing them to the predators while attempting to protect the young and virile in the center of the herd.

To put it bluntly, no matter how long you have been around, nor how much loyalty you have shown, this is a "what have you done for me lately" world and you will not survive if there is not something more behind your loyalty. No boss will sustain a member of the team which is no longer contributing. Nor should you allow yourself to become that person. It will be evident in these economically distressed times who is pulling their weight and who is relying on only loyalty to survive. It is those people who will fall first to the layoffs and you want to avoid that at all costs.

*"I'm indispensable. They can't find fault with me!"*

Avoiding overstepping one's boundaries is critical. This is a misstep that many a young manager or even seasoned executives take without sometimes realizing their folly. It is nice to believe that you are critical to an organization and it would make anyone feel good to truly be so important that no one would question your decisions, however, we are not invincible creatures. Even Steve Jobs was questioned for many years about his ability to run Apple – and although his is a good story now, time will only tell if his current empire will begin to crumble in the future. The ability we all have of making that assumption is inherent in our nature. We all strive to be the best, and it is wired in us to desire to attain that goal. But no one is perfect.

Niran was one of my supervisors early in my career. His lesson in overstepping one's boundaries and learning his true worth was difficult for not only his personal career, but also those of us on his team...

*Niran's Story*

Niran worked for years to make it to a leadership role within his firm. His department was one of the biggest and did most of the high-profile projects. And Niran knew that it was getting time for him to get another promotion. Unfortunately, his executive officer noticed that he was getting cocky. But without regard to his executive officer's comments that he should step carefully, Niran took on a new assignment from a client. But this was no ordinary assignment.

Niran knew the project somewhat outside of his team's skill level and would be controversial if it failed. And on top of that, he decided not to talk to the executive officer. Niran said to himself, *This is my company, I helped build it. They can't say anything even if they don't like it.* But that was not the case. Niran's executive officer allowed him to run with the project until it got into trouble. When the project began to fail because the project was outside of the firm's expertise, the executive officer stepped-in. Niran was removed from his position as department manager and in a fit of pride, he submitted his resignation.

There is no good animal to point at to say "here's how the animal world is cruel to its own that overstep their bounds" - because there is not. The alligator knows that it cannot kill the hippopotamus. The lion knows that to take the whole herd of bison down is very unwise. The snake even knows that to take on a dog or a cat is a last-defense. No animal is invincible. Every animal is vulnerable, and we people are the same, in all our life choices, including office politics.

If we much choose, the panda bear is perhaps the best example to look at when pondering the way which the jungle might tell us how to better understand the nature of office politics. Although I would never accuse the panda of overstepping it's boundaries or overreacting its limitations, it saddens me to point-out that the panda is indeed the victim of such overreaching – on the part of the humans. Now, I understand that humanity is a growing thing, but due to the dramatic suburbanization of the native panda territory, the panda population has dwindled to a point of near no-return.

Now, imagine if the panda had a benefactor, an animal that could protect the species of bear from us humans. Because we have overstepped our boundaries, our harm to the panda is virtually irreversible and any benefactor of the panda would certainly have gone after us with a bag of rat poison by now!

> *If only the human hadn't overstepped their boundaries into the habitat of the panda...then perhaps the panda would be a more successful animal.*
> Illustration 17

*"I work hard – that's good enough."*

Hard work is only a basic building block of success within today's corporate world. The rules which guide us demand that we not only work hard, but that good results be produced accordingly. If we cannot focus on many items, including working hard, we might as well quit now, because we're simply wasting time. My friend Rinzen learned this lesson well and took advantage of it when the opportunity arose.

<u>Rinzen's Story</u>

Rinzen worked hard for his firm, managing projects he was given and doing the production of his plan sets with pride. Rinzen thought he was doing well, but he never lifted a finger to market new work – that was being done for him. He never asked for the next promotion, he assumed that it would be handed to him.

But that wasn't the case. Another co-worker was given the next big promotion and the corresponding increase in pay. Rinzen felt hurt and mistreated. So, although he was concerned he would learn something he didn't want to know, he approached his boss. *What did I do wrong?* Rinzen asked. The boss' response: *Because you never pushed the boundaries and exhibited the desire to grow on your own, we didn't think you wanted the promotion.* Rinzen lost this battle. But he remembered the lesson he learned. The next time that a promotion was available, Rinzen had already laid the groundwork to get it by playing the office politics and showing his strong desire to grow. He got it the second time and is a happier man today.

Many birds work for weeks to build a nest. However, often they must leave the nest to find food, if even for just a moment. But while the nest is alone, it is vulnerable and can be easily destroyed by an invading snake looking to loot for eggs. The lesson that we can learn from the birds is to keep our work from being fruitless and empty by protecting the investments we have made. You do this not by just working hard, but working the political game and winning.

*Hard work does not always serve the bird best if the snake is waiting just a branch away to eat all the bird's precious eggs.*
Illustration 18

*"My boss loves me. Who cares if the other people in the office like me?!"*

Your boss is only your boss as long as he doesn't find another job, gets promoted or gets transferred. Someone else in your office could just as easily be your boss tomorrow as your current boss. Additionally, management comes and goes with mergers and acquisitions. If you bet the wrong horse, you will be cast out with the old horses.

And I don't recommend that you test it in these economically difficult times. Too many people have learned this lesson too late in their careers to start again and found themselves stuck with a new set of supervisors.

All we must do is to look at the cockroach to prove that this myth is a dangerous one to believe. The cockroach is well-built, with an exoskeleton which is virtually indestructible. The cockroach is designed for safely getting through some of the roughest environmental times. They may even be able to out-live a nuclear holocaust!

But the cockroach has one very big drawback – they are just gross! The cockroach is a despicably nasty little creature, living in darkness and breeding in massive quantities. It is obvious by the significant numbers of baby cockroaches that they love each other. But no one else likes them. The lesson we can learn is that while we might feel the love of our boss, certainly, if we become anything like the cockroach, certainly someone should be coming after us with a can of bug-spray, too!

The best human story I can tell you is about Tola, an acquaintance of mine from my very first job. I don't believe that Tola has ever really learned her lesson with regard to office politics.

*Tola's Story*

Tola had worked for Mr. C for several years. And when Mr. C was promoted, Tola was too. Tola assumed that because Mr. C had promoted her, that she was so valuable that it didn't really matter if she was a good boss or not to the team that Mr. C had just handed to her. So, Tola changed the rules for the position. She decided that she could go to have her nails and hair done during office hours without taking personal time; she decided that spending an hour every morning in the city library was acceptable; and she started regularly yelling at employees for minor mistakes. Her employees quickly came to hate Tola, but she didn't care. She would do anything that Mr. C asked of her, and that she would do with a smile, but when it came to the other people in the office, she couldn't care less.

And Mr. C didn't really care, either. Although several people complained, he thought Tola did a great job. So great, in fact, that when he was transferred to lead another region, he recommended that she be promoted to his position. But the firm had already asked another gentleman to fill Mr. C's role: Mr. A.

Needless to say, Tola was fired as soon as Mr. A found out these strange habits of hers. And, Mr. A wasn't very nice when a new firm called to find out Tola's references – Tola had a very hard time finding a comparable position, just because she had taken advantage of her last firm.

Tola's lesson is a hard one. And one we should all avoid. At no time should we consider that we are better than our co-workers, because they could just as easily be the new favorite tomorrow as we are today.

*"If I mind my own business, no one will bother me."*

This myth is very true. If you sit at your desk and work without becoming involved in the office environment around you, you will slowly rot. Or, you will be unprepared, vulnerable to attack and eaten alive.

Having no one bother you equates to: No one will bother with you. Being quiet and ignoring the outside world is a recipe for being forgotten and passed-over for the things that you want. So, don't fade into the background – learn to stand out!

I believed this myth when I first started working in the corporate world. However, after seeing what my co-worker Huy went through, I had no reason to believe that this myth was anything but false.

*Huy's Story*

Huy worked very hard every day. He came to work on time and left when his work was done. But he got a very bad reputation for not being very friendly. Because Huy was always working at his desk and was very quiet, his co-workers became somewhat afraid of him and slowly, his whole day narrowed to only those people brave enough to walk into his office and start a conversation on their own.

Huy toiled away, working for five years in the same position, the only person that spoke to him on a regular basis was his boss. Huy never complained when he wasn't promoted, until eventually, his family needed him to attain a promotion. At that point, Huy really had to fight to earn the promotion. His bosses just didn't think that Huy deserved it since they hadn't seen him "show an interest" before that date. It was another full year before Huy could convince them, although by changing his ways, he eventually did.

Just like we should do in the concrete jungle, animals walk cautiously in the jungle. They mind their businesses – but they interact with the other animals significantly, observing their surroundings and observing the actions of the animals around them.

*By running from danger, the deer can lessen the likelihood that they will become the meal.*
Illustration 19

When morning dawns in Africa, the deer prays, "Dear Lord, make me run faster than the fastest lion."

And the lion prays, "Dear Lord, make me run faster than the slowest deer."

The truth of the matter is, when morning comes, you better be running! This is so applicable to the corporate world! And as a successful executive, you must know it better than everyone else that you have to constantly keep moving to stay ahead of others!

## Fight or Flight

## When to put up your dukes or cut and run

The white-tailed deer works in a strong team to warn the herd of impending danger – flying in the face of that danger when only one senses it. And this flexibility and apparent readiness to run has kept it alive and safe in many situations. But just as quickly, one must be prepared to turn and fight in the office jungle, but you are the only one to decide for you if that is within your abilities.

There are strengths and weaknesses of each person depending on the situation and your ability to fight or fly may hinge on the situation's timing or grounds. Everyone has a bad day, but avoiding failure through logical decision making is easy if you follow your instincts. First, you must learn your personal strength and weaknesses, then embark upon an effort to ensure that you play on both. For example, the komodo dragon never has to worry if his meal will get away. One of his very strong strengths is that the dragon can bite a cow (just one bite) and the cow may struggle and flee, but the bite is so venomous and so terribly stinky that the dragon can kill the cow with that one bite – and find the carcass later with no issue due to the hideous smell!

The crux of winning political battles is finding the right grounds and establishing the right timing. And if you approach each battle with a respect for each of these things, you are sure to succeed. So, when fighting is the only way, recall that timing and grounds are key and consider both before charging ahead. The last thing you want to do is be blindsided by an unknown because someone else thought of these things and you did not.

*Finding the right battle ground is not impossible*

The Lion is not the king when in the water. In the river it is the crocodile and in the oceans, the sharks. For people it is the same. If you are facing confrontation and need to find a battle ground, choose wisely. You know that dressing-down someone in a conference call is sometimes what you want to do. We've all had that feeling and know that it would immediately been satisfying. However, we all also know that to do so may cost us more than we could ever enjoy the moment. So, you choose your battle ground. Be it a one-on-one or a meeting with the human resources department to clarify something with a co-worker, it is up to you to choose where you will do battle.

Therefore, in playing the political game, make sure that the battle ground is a favorable one on which you can combat and thrive.

*The shark can no more be the king of the bathroom floor than the lion be the king of the ocean.*
Illustration 20

*Deciding when the right time to make your move*

The animals often choose to fight or to run based on timing. An animal simply will step back and choose to fight another day if they feel that the timing is not right. This occurs for them each day of their lives. In winter, clearly animals with a thick and heavy coat will survive better than those which are equipped only for the heat of the day, and vice versa in the summer. So, an animal that doesn't have a heavy fur to throw-on around September is going to migrate south, while others can stay and tough it out.

The same goes for office politics. For restructuring and downsizing season etc, a financially trained or autocratic leader may be better suited to succeeding where a marketing or people oriented leader would not. Keep that in mind as you choose when to pick your fight and when to back down. Timing may mean the difference between defeat and victory.

*Manny's Story*

Manny was continually put-down in front of his team members by one of their number. Although he was the project manager, this young man always seemed to find fault with Manny and his design, leaving him with little options to defend himself. Several times, he had tried to contradict the young man, but he feared getting into a greater conflict with him in front of the other team members.

Then, one day, the young man pointed out another of Manny's mistakes in a meeting. Manny was very frustrated, but he saw a flaw in the young man's thinking. Then, it dawned on Manny! He had found the right battle ground and the right time to make his move. So, he pressed the advantage and took the opportunity to not only teach the young man, and the whole team, a new technique, but to also show the young man that he did know what he was doing. And when he finished, a new respect dawned in several of the team member's eyes.

Manny started looking at the office environment with a new view. He took every opportunity that the young man presented and turned it around into an opportunity to learn – if not for the young man, then for others, often asking the young man to teach the team how to do some of the techniques he espoused. Manny realized that the young man had not been trying to upstage him, but rather had been reaching out for help in understanding the tricks of their trade. Manny's new attitude created a whole new working relationship between them and now, that young man is Manny's go-to-guy for almost all of his best projects.

*Career-building is not a sprint – it's a marathon*

**It does not matter how slowly you go so long as you do not stop.**

**~ *Confucius***

Illustration 27

The lack of long-term planning has become rampant in our world-market today. This phenomenon has become a real problem as many people are searching for a short-term solution, and avoiding the long-term solution because it will require more thought and more investment of time or energy. Clearly this is evident in the American shake-up of Bear Stearns, Fannie Mae. Freddie Mac, Lethman Brothers. Great catastrophe for the world-wide economy could have been avoided if only those brokers and bankers who worked on commission would have looked to the future and seen past the bonuses that could be had in the immediate. Because these people (and many others at places like Enron and other big firms before them even) looked only to the near-rewards and ignored the long-term gains, the American economy was fragile and eager to fail. In 2005 to 2007, if the American lending and banking industry had focused on the long-term solution, perhaps the American economy would still be stable.

And this is evident in Asian society as well. For example, there was a lot of bad publicity when Ms. Lee Bee Wah, President of the Singapore Table Tennis Association sacked the coach after the 2008 Olympics match that led to a silver medal for the Singapore women's top table tennis champion. The timing was bad as this was the first time that Singapore had won an Olympics medal since independence. It was supposed to be a time to celebrate. Instead, the poor sensitivity and bad political maneuvering attracted a lot of bad press. If Ms. Bee Wah had stopped to consider the repercussions of her actions, perhaps she could have saved much face and respect from the table tennis enthusiast community and the political scene.

This type of short-term view has had a strong effect on the economy, but most importantly, on our own careers. Take Tara for example:

*Tara's Story*

Tara led the pack when it came to winning work. But as the economy started to turn for the worse, Tara received quite a shock. Although her bonuses were tied to the number of projects she received, they were also tied to her accounts receivable. While the economy was high, she was able to pull in many projects without regard to the quality of the client and their ability to pay in tight financial situations.

But, when the economy was down, her bonuses were down since her clients couldn't pay and on top of that, in the bad economy, her ability to win projects was diminished. Tara lost face with her partners and her ability to maintain her practice was in question. Tara had to do a complete turnaround of her practice and focus on a new type of client, accepting the diminished number of projects she could win. Her bonuses have been better since she switched direction, but they have not yet reached the heights they had been previously.

The lesson we can look to the animals for is best illustrated by the cheetah. The cheetah is very quick to sprint when necessary, but takes its time to stalk its prey and makes a decision to run at full speed only when it knows that it will be successful. If the cheetah tried to run-down the gazelle from too far away, the gazelle would easily out-pace the cheetah in a longer run. The cheetah's body is only built to race at high speeds for short distances. And he knows that, so he thinks long-term and rather than just sprinting toward everything he sees and losing all of his energy in the first run, he bides his time and waits until the closest, slowest gazelle is available, then he starts his run.

The only animal that might give us a different view of this concept of long-term choices might be the human. In order to ensure the species survived hard times and flourished during good times, the human species has made changes – like standing on two legs and learning to use tools. These tools included fire, spears, axes, and all of the further tools that evolved from those basics. These may seem like trivial things since we have certainly elevated ourselves above the concept of simple "tools" that our ancestors used. However, if we look at the example critically, we can see that truly, the most forward-thinking species is the human. We see the changes as they were carried from the cave to the field, from the field to the warehouse and so on and so forth until you find each of us attached to a computer. Based on this review, one could say that the human animal is the most politically savvy example we could look to for guidance.

## The Human Animal

## Our Good and Bad Animal Instincts

The Human is an animal, there is no doubt. We can believe that we come from a great creator God or you can believe that we are evolved from apes. Whatever your belief, it is easy to see that we once lived side-by-side with the animals and are a part of them as much as they are a part of us.

Our history as an animal gives us some significant advantages in that we have some very deep-set instincts that will tell us how to react in a political situation. Simply look at our children – they interact with each other on a constant basis, often making mistakes, but on the main interacting in a very politically instinctive manner. Now, I am not suggesting that you behave like a two-year-old during a board meeting, however, I am saying that somewhere deep inside, we have some cues and some inclinations that, if we listen to them, might serve us on the political stage.

Our innate instincts serve to guide us through many tough situations that we face through life. We all know not to eat excrement (unless you happen to be on a horrible reality television show) and we all know how to react to a baby's cry. These and many other involuntary responses are built into our psyche as a human. In theory, we should be able to translate these instincts into actions when we enter a politically-charged office situation. Children are the perfect example. They all are born with the knowledge of how to cry to receive attention, hold their breath underwater, and various other responses. Children's behavior can be directly linked to the evolution of the human being and we can clearly see how they act is linked to the way that we act. We can break this down into five different caricatures which I'll label: Breathing, Toy-Taking, Biting, Acting and Sharing.

*Breathing*

Imagine a single moment without breath. No baby born which continues to live can do without that first breath and every subsequent one. From the moment they are separated from their mothers by the ominous cutting of the umbilical cord, the little baby forces oxygen through its lips and the process of breathing begins. This is an instinct that only very few babies are born without – and those often do not survive, and cannot survive without technology.

As adults, we continue to do the same. We are forced to breathe continually. Even when we intentionally hold our breath, we gasp at the end of our deprivation and the process resumes without end.

Some behaviors in the office are like breathing. Sometimes, we go through processes of posturing and jockeying for power without even realizing our actions. We meet a person, greet them, and then perhaps the conscious political movements kick-in. However, in those first few moments, certainly we are still working on that same political posturing. It is all in how we dress, carry ourselves, and address the other person and body language. If one or many other things are out of order in the other person, you would immediately notice it, and they will likewise notice any inconsistencies in your initial presentation.

These unconscious responses make up a significant portion of how we determine our following behavior. And we perform the analysis of how to behave without even thinking. We simply perform the reflex analysis and upon determining how to initially behave, we then allow the higher-reflexes or more conscious efforts to take effect.

*Toy-Taking*

Toy-taking is one of the semi-unconscious efforts which is also an instinct for which children are often admonished. Toy-taking is as simple as the term implies. Toy-taking is the act of one greedy child taking a toy from another child that was unwilling to share. My child is the perfect example. My little girl used to be found on multiple occasions throughout the day taking another child's toy at school. This is most certainly not a habit I have taught her. She is simply re-allocating what she perceives to be a resource to her own stores (her hands). If the reallocation is noted, a fight may ensue. Or, if the taking goes unnoticed, the behavior is rewarded by possession of the toy.

*Taking a toy or resource away from someone not only hurts that person, but it attracts attention and can cause serious upset in the organization.*
Illustration 21

Children can be seen doing this to each other throughout their days, and if left unadmonished, I am certain that they would continue to do so throughout their lives (thank goodness my child is not the only one!). This is why we admonish them – to break them of the habit.

However, I contend that we are never truly broken of the habit and will revert to toy-taking often in the office situation. This behavior is different in the office, though. Certainly, one cannot reach across the conference room table, take your opponent's folder and stick out one's tongue at him as you do so. This would simply not be acceptable behavior. But there are other toy-taking techniques which are acceptable in the workplace.

In the office, we consider it resource re-allocation – the same as the child. Only, in the office, we can think of it in terms of getting a promotion over another person or competing for an office with a window. We often clearly see toy-taking when we are the victim, but often do not recognize it when we take toys from others. I would consider this "unconscious" toy-taking.

Unconscious toy-taking can consist of "stepping on someone's toes" or many other phrases that describe the act of infringing on another person's domain. The act of toy-taking by any name though is the same. Within the office environment, if one person, even accidentally, takes the responsibilities of another unrightfully or over-shadow's another person's triumphs inappropriately, that effectively is toy-taking. By doing this, many bosses drive employees to find another firm and many co-workers find themselves at-odds with each other.

*Deena's Story*

Deena felt she had the world at her fingertips. Around the corner, she knew that there was promotion and advancement awaiting her – all the things she had worked hard to attain for many years. But her boss had a poor meeting with their main client which ended poorly. During this meeting, the client admonished Deena's boss for several mistakes that were made, but had been inevitable due to the client's lack of communication. Rather than defend the choices that the team had made, Deena's boss simply folded under the pressure.

When he returned to the office, her boss was so concerned that they might lose the project, he reacted by doing as much of the work himself as he possibly could, taking away all of the responsibilities that he would previously have given Deena. Deena was stripped of her previous triumphs and her hopes of promotion were quickly dashed.

It wasn't long before Deena started looking for another position, since she no longer felt that she had an opportunity for advancement. When she turned-in her resignation, her boss expressed that he was blind-sided and never would have suspected that she would walk-away. And when she explained how hurt she had been that he had taken all of her hard-won accomplishments from her, he divulged that he hadn't even been conscious of the fact that he had done so. He tried to make amends, but it was too late. Deena had already accepted the other position, and as a result, both she and her boss missed-out on a great opportunity.

*Biting*

Biting is the same way. Children bite as a way to express emotion and as a way to exert ownership or control over another person or child. This is a similar behavior to animals with regard to mouthing and exploring the world through their lips. We've all experienced either the puppy's mouthing of our hand or the bite of a younger sibling – or perhaps we were the one's doing the biting. Either way, young human children and young animals all bite during one of the stages of growth.

Though we can't even remotely suggest that within the office world that biting is a common occurrence, I do contend that as adults we have found more efficient (and less slobbery) ways to bite at each other. The main way that I believe we exhibit the same biting behavior as children is through our use of tone and how we 'snip' or make sharp remarks toward one another. These adult-bites hurt just as much as the ones that leave tiny little teeth-dimples on your skin. And they are as effective as a child's bite at exploring the world, expressing emotion, and exerting control over another person.

But this adult biting is no more acceptable to the common populace. An office-biter is often assumed to be playing bad politics and looked-down upon as providing only unconstructive criticism. Just as there are admonishments that are paid to a biting child, office-biters are admonished for their poor behavior. And although there is a perception that some of the quick quips and small snips are harmless to others (especially if said outside of the hearing of the subject) and may relieve stress for the biter, these statements are quite painful to the team and the subject, making others (which may not even be involved) ask "So what does he/she say about me?" This becomes a poison to the team that will eat the team from the inside.

<u>Xun's Story</u>

When Xun came to work at this organization, a lot of things were different than what he would have liked them to be. His outlook was optimistic, though. He knew he was a hard-worker and that he could be the best technical expert that the firm had ever seen. But during meetings, Xun had a very bad habit. He would lash-out at people unexpectedly and for actions that were either not within their control or simple things that could have been easily changed.

*Biting hurts and can cause massive disruptions in the office jungle!*
*Illustration 22*

Xun was, as a result, considered hard to work with. No matter how hard someone worked, always, when they discussed the deliverable or the next steps, Xun would unerringly admonish them in an aggressive and un-defendable way. It didn't take long until Xun was considered to be a poor team player. In addition, those people who did have the unfortunate luck to work with Xun became paranoid and were continually looking over their shoulders and suspicious of any statement that might be made about themselves and damage their reputation. This made the team disintegrate and begin being dismantled by losses to other firms and transfers to other teams. It wasn't very long until his supervisors noticed the trend, but it was too late. Without the ability to work in a team, Xun was shunned when promotion opportunities arose and slowly, he discovered that he would never move-up in his organization.

The greatest detriment to the organization that comes from a biter is the poison that is spread in the form of paranoia. This paranoia can rip through an organization like a virus and is not easily quieted once it has taken hold. This is a classic example of poorly-played politics and can bring failure to an entire firm if not stopped before it spreads.

*Once bitten by a snake, you are even frightened by a rope that resembles a snake.*
          ~ *Proverb*

Illustration 27

*Acting*

Acting, also known as lying, is a tactic children take without even realizing that they do so. A child will lie, whether it be hiding an act that they know they should not do or answering a question adversely to achieve a means that they want but otherwise would not be able to attain. The children don't learn this, it is an innate characteristic that they cannot change. As children age, this lying is admonished and buried – hidden from everyday activities, but the ability to do so lies latent in every one.

This behavior blossoms in some as acting which they take to become a career. However, we are each an actor on the stage of politics. If we can see ourselves as actors, when we step back and think about ourselves rationally, we can see the truth of the statement. We each act on the stage of our office – just like Shakespeare's famous statement: "All the world is a stage and all of us actors and actresses." He's absolutely right. We each act on the stage of the day and although there are no scripts or directors, we each are the actors moving about and making our debuts before the audience of our peers.

This is evident from the personality differences we each see between the person at work and the person in your home life. Each of us maintains these two different personalities and, one could say, that neither is wholly real, although surely they are each a version of the other. Unfortunately, the reality is that either personality could be real – and the other is that personality we exhibit as an act. However, if we had to determine which was more real, most people would pick the home-personality as the real one. So, that would mean that each person within the office is an actor.

*Lei's Story*

Lei had worked hard to gain a position within her firm which was very influential. To get there, she had to learn how to be aggressive and how to argue strongly to achieve her desires. She even had to learn to seek healthy conflict by taking stances opposing her own desires in some situations in order to find the best solutions for the situation. Additionally, Lei was decisive and would attack any problem head-on, never avoiding only taking action to solve. All of this behavior seemed to come naturally to Lei, and she needed very little coaching to learn these tactics.

But her personality at home was significantly different. She never argued with her spouse. She always took guidance from her friends and never did anything but follow. Even with her children, she would often worry so much that she never made a decision and her spouse had to step-in on many occasions just to give her basic direction. This wasn't a problem for Lei on a normal day, but she was frustrated that in her work life she was in control and able to take charge, but in her home live she was weak and always under the sway of someone else.

Lei thought about trying to change her personality at home, but really, that was the way that she wanted to behave, that's how she got along best with her husband and friend, and she felt that her choices had been right. However, just recognizing that she did believe in the choices that she had made and that she wanted to be the way she was made her better understand herself.

*Sharing*

Sharing is a trait that we may think comes with adulthood, but I assure you that the first sharing occurred between children. Although children are often viewed as selfish and unthinking, they have many of the quality traits that make up an adult – including sharing. In many instances, I have found my daughter to be very generous to other children in her class. If she can be found giving another child a portion of her cookie when theirs is missing from their lunchbox, then certainly sharing is an innate activity. And although children can be selfish, there are times when they see another child crying or another child which is unhappy and, a child can be very compassionate and provide a hug or share a toy. And this carries with us through adulthood, becoming more and more of a trait we can rely on to get us through every day.

## Min's Story

Min was, at first, a very timid project manager. She kept to herself for the most part, only interacting with other team-leaders when she was required. Min ran her team well, but noticed that one of the other team-leaders, Ami, often struggled with the technical execution of her projects. After seeing Ami struggle for several days on a particularly important project, Min pulled her aside after a meeting and offered to help Ami, although at first she wasn't sure how to help. Ami was very excited and immediately they began brainstorming. Throughout the conversation, they noted many differences in their teams, but after a short discussion on the techniques that Ami's team was using for computer aided design, Min determined that what Ami's team needed was a specialty training that Min's team had attended several months before. Ami was more than willing to try anything.

Min helped Ami convince their boss that Ami's team would benefit from the training, then she helped Ami get it scheduled – and helped Ami with her workload while her team attended. Ami was so grateful that when it came time to recommend bonuses, Ami spoke specifically to their boss about Min's extraordinary efforts to help her team be more productive. Min's boss was very impressed by Ami's openness – but he was far more impressed that Min had stepped-in, shared her expertise and experience, thus effectively saving Ami's team from sure failure. Both Min and Ami received significantly higher bonuses that year and made long-term strides toward a partnership between their two teams.

By reviewing some elements of childhood behavior and how adults act-out these same innate habits, we really can see that there are certain responses that are instinctive to our species. Clearly, because this behavior is ingrained in our species, we can see that office politics are inevitable for the human animal. As long as we work with people there will be jockeying for resources, power and control on a daily basis. The key to success is learning how to assimilate into the office politics environment without being eaten alive and learning how to defend one's turf without becoming a pest or a nuisance.

We can learn some of these tactics by getting back to our jungle-roots and looking at the animals for guidance. And because we're imbedded with some of the animal instincts, we can compare ourselves to the animals easily. And with this comparison, we can translate to establishing a typical stance for our use on any given day, a useful tactic for maneuvering any concrete jungle.

## A Favorite Animal

## How choosing one can help you

The best way to look for the true tips that the animal world can give us is to pick a favorite animal to emulate on a relatively regular basis. By modifying your behavior to follow the tactics of a favorite animal with situational changes, you can easily find a solution to even the stickiest of situations. So, how do you pick a favorite animal? We can break this down into three questions:

*What is the state of your firm and what animal would thrive in that environment?*

*What is your underlying personality and what animal would most resemble it?*

*What animal would most resemble where you want to grow?*

Once you've answered these three questions, you should have a pretty good idea of the right animal to fit your needs. But how do you apply the techniques that these animals can teach us?

The easiest way to apply the tactics that the animals can teach us is to consider the jungle-situation which is most similar to that you are in and apply the animal's responses to the concrete jungle. So, for example, say we've decided that the mustang (wild horse) is our favorite animal. Knowing ahead of the situation that this is going to be our animal-example will allow us to rely on their tactics naturally. So, let's run through some examples:

<u>Concrete Jungle:</u> You encounter another manager jockeying for the same choice project as you.

The mustang's situation: Another young mustang has intruded in the prime mustang's herd and seeks the attention of the prime mustang's favorite female.

How the mustang reacts: The prime mustang challenges the new one, putting himself between the favored female and the new mustang. By placing his claim early in the situation, the young male will see that there is already a dominating male in the herd and will either move on or join the herd, but regardless, the situation will be diffused.

Applying the mustang's lesson: Claim what you want early-on and others will know what you want. Often, people don't realize that what they pursue is even the object of another's desire. If you exhibit that you truly desire something, often the other person which pursues it will relinquish their claim without any conflict.

*The mustang can be a good example for us to see how a favored animal might give us guidance in our daily office interactions.*
Illustration 23

*Concrete Jungle:* You have an employee that is too aggressive and is trying to upstage you.

The mustang's situation: A young mustang in the prime mustang's herd has challenged the prime mustang to a fight for supremacy.

How the mustang reacts: First, the prime mustang claims his herd – similar to the first example. If that doesn't work, then conflict may be the only way to solve the situation. The prime mustang will paw the air and bell his challenge, showing his dominance through a show of strength. Often that may be the end of the confrontation for the mustang herd as the younger mustang will see the challenge for what it is and leave before even the first blow.

Applying the mustang's lesson: As we learned in earlier chapters, we sometimes have to face conflict, but unlike the animals, we can't paw the air and fight for resolution, we have to fight with words and civility. However, the mustang shows us that a show of strength will often solve a situation before true conflict must be fought. You can have a show of strength simply by telling the new employee that you don't appreciate their advances. Often that new employee doesn't even realize that he's doing anything to make you uncomfortable and will stop upon your discussion.

*Concrete Jungle:*  You have a new CEO starting and he wants to have lunch with you to "get to know you."

>The mustang's situation:  A new filly has become the dominant female in the herd.

>How the mustang reacts:  The prime mustang takes the opportunity and presses any advantage that he can get from the new filly. His stance will be one of acceptance and trying to help the filly with her decisions – even from the beginning. The mustang does not fight the new filly and won't challenge her, but rather accepts this new change in his herd and carries-on without concern.

>Applying the mustang's lesson:  When leadership changes occur that you are not in control of, you should accept it and press your new advantage. If the new CEO wants to meet with you – perfect! Get to know him if he wants to get to know you. Certainly if he is interested in you, then he's not looking to challenge you, but rather is looking to work with you. Most people would feel threatened by a new CEO's advances in this manner, but if you go in with a cool head and approach the situation as a new one that you can take advantage of, surely you can make more of it than your peers.

*Concrete Jungle:* Your newest employee has just saved you from a potential failure on a big project.

> The mustang's situation: A new filly has joined the herd and brought them news of a sweet pasture behind her.
>
> How the mustang reacts: The mustang is going to want to reward this new filly by giving her precedence in the herd. He'll take advantage of the information he gets from the new filly and then he'll give her his attention and thanks. However, at no time would the mustang disrupt the natural order of his herd. He cannot over-thank this new filly, but rather will simply allow her into the herd and thank her appropriately, then go on with business as usual.
>
> Applying the mustang's lesson: If you have an employee who has done you this great service, you should justly reward them. But like the mustang, just because your newest employee has provided you with some service, you must temper your thanks and make sure that you do not upset the natural order of your office. Just as the mustang takes great care to ensure that his herd is not disrupted, you must do the same. While praise is good and shows great character of a strong leader to be able to praise someone, certainly too much praise can unsettle the other employees within the team. The mustang teaches us caution and judiciousness in our praise and this is a wise lesson to take.

*Concrete Jungle:* You have just been assigned a new project but it's too much for your team to successfully complete.

> The mustang's situation: The herd has just come upon a great pasturage that is too much for the herd to eat – and besides, they must move on soon.
>
> How the mustang reacts: The mustang leads his herd in eating their fill, but he is sure to leave much for the next herd – even possibly belling a call for those herds which might be nearby. The key thing to note is that he doesn't destroy the pasture, he eats what his herd can, then leaves the rest, effectively sharing it with those that would come next. When he leaves, he will not defile the sweet grasses or try to take it with him – he can't, he doesn't have opposable thumbs or backpacks with which to pack it away during their journey. That would be foolish. The mustang simply leaves the pasturage and shares it with the next herd.
>
> Applying the mustang's lesson: Share. Which may mean asking for help and sharing immediately, but may also mean doing what you can and sharing at the end what you cannot. Sharing, as we noted in the last chapter, is an innate human ability, but certainly the animals also do this. And by playing clean politics and sharing when you can, you will win the gratitude of those around you. The sign of a true leader is one which can admit a weakness and turn it into an opportunity.

*When to change to a different favorite animal*

The mustang doesn't do so well against a lion – the lion will simply win. So, when you know you've encountered another, stronger animal, rather than fold and walk away, switching to a more appropriate animal would be the most successful tactic. How can you know when this change is necessary? How do you make this transition naturally?

Being aware that you must be asking these questions of yourself during each situation and then answering them honestly to yourself can be the difference between a leader and a follower. Recognizing that a change in your typical behavior is necessary can give you an edge that others may not have. It is this flexibility that can save you in hard times or make you shine in an otherwise mild victory.

So, keep in mind that no single animal is the only animal that might guide your decisions in the political office world. The concrete jungle is an ever-changing, ever-transitioning and a successful player will change themselves with it.

*No single animal will be the perfect one for all situations – learn to be flexible and perhaps you won't be the lion's dinner...*
Illustration 24

## **When Nothing Stays the Same**

## **How to deal with transition in a situation and more**

Because the political office is ever-changing and ever-transitioning, and because you need to be the same to be successful, it stands to reason that understanding this transition is a key attribute that should be studied. Often, even in the same situation, one can go from being on the defensive end of a conversation to being on the offensive – and vice-versa!

So how do we recognize the changes? And how do we respond to this transition in a single situation, on a week-to-week basis, or on a longer term situation when your whole world turns upside-down?

There are some simple answers for each of these questions for which the animals may give us some guidance.

*A Single Confrontation*

For each situation there is the potential for change, be it abrupt or gradual which may be for or against your cause. The key is to take advantage of the situation, whichever way it begins to change. The animals do this well. If a lion is wandering the jungle in search of food and comes upon the snake, the lion knows that to play with the snake and ignore the risk that he may be bitten would be irrational. So, rather than play with the snake, he avoids it – and the snake may do the same. This may change how the lion moved through the jungle on that day. Certainly, should there be sudden change in the path of your day in the office, the rules of the concrete jungle would require that you change your ways in the same manner. My co-worker Hajime learned this lesson recently.

*Even the lion is wary around the snake. You must take the same approach and be wary of the obstacles that you may find in the office jungle.*
*Illustration 25*

<u>Hajime's Story</u>

Working hard was nothing new to Hajime. He worked hard at everything – including working at office politics. He would read all of the famous books regarding cheese and war, trying hard to understand how best to maneuver in this dangerous environment. However, he wasn't quite prepared for what befell him one day during a meeting. He had come to the meeting prepared to present an innovative idea that his team had formulated for dealing with a particularly difficult project.

But when Hajime started the discussion, a person who Hajime believed to be a quiet and unobtrusive audience turned into a real adversary. Hajime was surprised by this change in this man's attitude and might have been sidetracked by the mere awkwardness. This new adversary was attacking Hajime's ideas at every turn, something that Hajime never suspected. However, Hajime had seen something very similar happen to one of his fellow co-workers and that situation had ended poorly, affecting her for a long time. So, Hajime decided to deal with this change in a different manner and overcome it with his confidence and his wit.

Hajime stopped trying to layout his new plan and began attacking the problem from a different perspective, selling his plan by backing his audience into the decision themselves. Hajime lead his prey into the trap and then sprung it around them all-unknowing! Hajime made his audience believe that they had come-up with the proposed action! And when they asked how they would implement it, Hajime was already prepared to do so! He came out looking like a hero, even through his adversary would have had it otherwise when the meeting opened. But if Hajime had ignored the change and not acknowledged that his footing was dangerous, certainly the situation would never have ended so well.

*A Week-To-Week Basis*

Sometimes changes don't just occur in the situation, but occur on a week-to-week basis which may be more gradual or more sudden than situational changes.

<u>*Kiamu's Story*</u>

Kiamu was hard working and politically conscious of his behavior on a fairly consistent basis. Had he been having trouble focusing and staying politically conscious for longer than a week, he might never have noticed the changes that were occurring around him in his office. Certainly there were a lot of folks in his department that were missing the changes around them and they were being picked-off one by one. This is something that Kiamu noticed and determined that he didn't want to be a part of. So, Kiamu took action. Although the changes happening around them were subtle – a new department head here, the layoff of one or two people there, and the shifting of resources from one project to another, Kiamu was keen to them and shifted those things he was in control of to serve the new goals better.

At first, Kiamu changed the attitude he took toward collections, since that appeared to be a new goal to his leaders. Then, Kiamu focused on getting his bills out earlier to his clients, billing more as the work was done than after it was done. Kiamu also spent more time with his clients, seeking to increase their sales and reduce the amount of change-orders required by poor communication. Although his previous behavior fit well with the corporate concept before, now his behavior fit perfectly with the new ideas being espoused by his leaders. It took Kiamu three or four weeks, but eventually, though his gradual changes, he was able to make the bosses notice that his focuses were the same as their new ones. And by standing out from the herd, he was rewarded well.

For Kiamu, noticing the changes and taking effective action over the following weeks was exactly what it took to lead him to success. But what happens when your whole world turns upside-down? What is the effective approach when nothing seems sure anymore?

*When Your Whole World Tilts*

In the jungle, there are natural disasters such as floods, drought etc. Even the strongest of animals can die in any one of these situations, but the most flexible animals, ones that adapt to the changes are able to survive. But it all depends on the situation if the animal is the right animal to make that transition occur. And sometimes, the jungle is just too harsh for even the most flexible.

Animals are known for moving to greener pastures. They are sensitive to the changes in their environment. For example, animals seem to know of an impending tsunami or earthquake will move to safer grounds. Even the human animal can be heard to do this – when more primitive peoples were contacted after the great tsunami in Indonesia several years ago, they were said to have very few lives lost because their elders felt the tsunami coming and herded the entire tribes to higher ground.

> *By putting his ear to the ground and listening for change, the elephant can detect the tsunami in time to move away from the danger.*
> Illustration 26

But sometimes, knowing that change is coming is just not enough. What the Americans deem as the "Great Depression" is one of those instances in which there is no way to save yourself, no matter how flexible you are. When the American stock market crashed in the late 1920's, no one would have suspected that it would be a total economic meltdown for that country. And even now, if there is not dramatic change in the way that Americans do business and if they can't resist looking only to the immediate future as opposed to the more long-term economic well-being of their nation, certainly they will fall into that same trap again. Unfortunately, because of the intricately inter-woven nature of the world market, it may be that America will bring down more than just their country this time.

The same can be said for the office scene.

We need to be politically sensitive to the changes that might occur around us. This may include changes of management, or ownership, but it also may be changes in the marketplace or the competitive dynamics of your specific region. For example, as hard-hit as some of the coastal areas of the United States have been in the past year, some regions of the US have been barely touched, such as Dallas, and now many firms are hedging their bets by shifting operations to these areas which appear to be "safer" than others.

You must be prepared to do the same. Only vigilance may save you from being unemployed in times of economic hardship or a downturn in your business type. However, you can't change the economy and you can't force customers to start buying your product. So how do you make the changes necessary to survive? And how can you be prepared when something hits you that are too big to deal with directly?

My friend Masa had a very wise story to share with regard to changes that might be too big to handle.

*Masa's Story*

Masa built a practice from the ground up. He had never done the type of work that he was suddenly doing, but in the good-times of the late 1990's economy, he could market many potential clients and enough client's would accept him in order for Masa to make his goals. However, as his business (commercial airlines) went south after the attack on the World Trade Centers in 2001, he began to see that his fortunes had fallen, too. While he could market many clients, seemingly without end, fewer and fewer were willing to take a bet with someone less experienced. Soon, Masa was missing his goals and there didn't seem to be anywhere to turn for help. Masa knew that his bosses would be approaching him soon and the conversation wouldn't be good. He also knew that if he didn't change his practice, or if his practice didn't change, he wouldn't be able to disagree with his bosses.


So, Masa began examining his situation and options. He had a degree in Business Administration from a prominent university. This was a very versatile degree in which he could do virtually anything. But when he had chosen this career, it had been for the wrong reasons. He didn't choose something that would provide him with long-term benefits, just something that would get him a few dollars quickly. When he entered this practice, he had assumed that the firm would pursue a more senior practice builder with experience in this arena within a year or two, but that hadn't been the case.

Masa decided that he had overstayed his welcome in this practice and that he should have chosen something that would provide him with longer-term benefits, the career that he had walked away from when he came to this one. So, Masa was expecting it when the day came (and it was very quickly after he had done his own assessment) that his bosses approached him about leaving this firm. Masa accepted that he couldn't change the economy at the time, couldn't have stopped the terrorists from hijacking three planes in America, and he couldn't force the few clients to buy from him instead of the more experienced firms.

Because he had been prepared and was ready to make this change, he left his firm far more gracefully than he had been anticipated to by his bosses. Masa quickly transitioned to a new business type that was still growing strong, but one in which he had several years of experience. He chose more wisely this time by finding a senior practice builder that was looking for a young professional to train so that he could retire in the coming years. Masa built on this senior professional's experience and had a far more successful practice in the end than he would ever have been able to build at his previous firm.

Although disappointed that he had to make a transition, he was able to salvage himself, if not that specific career. He did go without a job for several months, but because he knew this was coming, he had saved as much as possible and made some changes in his personal life that allowed him this opportunity. If he had not been prepared, surely Masa would have been in a bind and would have had to make a very short-sighted decision in order to just put food on the table for his children.

In today's tough business world, with the world moving toward a global recession which may last for years, performance is mandatory but it is not enough to keep you moving forward – and may not be enough to keep you in your position. We need to flow with the system and culture, working with the office ecosystem. You cannot ignore the winds of change.

You must always be prepared, because even playing politics may not guarantee success. Your company can be acquired, merged or closed down – and even if you know it's coming, you may not be able to stop it or change the outcome. One needs to be prepared and be flexible, even if that means being flexible outside your firm. You should always remember that you may have to be a free agent at some point in the future. By being financially over-committed, you may be backing yourself into a corner. Masa saved himself by putting some savings aside and avoiding the poor financial habits that so many people get into. You can also have the same problem if you are narrow-viewed and refuse to learn new skills or adjust your business model. By learning multiple skills, or building your toolbox of abilities, you can open yourself to have more possible streams of income.

### Appropriate Action –

### A summary of the lessons we can learn

No matter how many tools are in your toolbox or sources of income you have, you will not always know the right move to make or the right stance to take. No single stance will always be the right political stance. The key lesson here is to learn from the animals and take the information they can give you and put it to your use.

For example, bears hibernate in winters but store-up great amounts of fat to make it through those lean months. From them we can learn to build-up good will with our co-workers even during the good times so that in the bad times we have more good will backlog – and we can learn that saving can be the key to surviving economic difficulties, so we should always be working toward increasing our savings.

Another example would be the eagle. Eagles soar with the winds and not against it, making the most of the fickle breezes to carry them high to find prey. The eagle will not fight the wind, knowing that to do so would force him to plummet to the ground. Likewise, we should accept, gracefully, any uplift that comes to us throughout our career. We should use the opportunities that are presented to us, even if they might not be exactly what you desire in the moment.

Every animal will have something to teach us, be it something small that might influence a single interaction or something significant which can influence one's entire career. We need to read into what the animal's tactics are to learn the valuable lessons they can share. Acknowledge that we all need to work on our personal development and take the lessons the animals can give us and improve yourself.

Know the situation and move with the tides. Adapt with the changing circumstances and situations. Determine the specific issues, problems and then determine the appropriate solutions. No problem is so great that it cannot be overcome – and there are many solutions.

We should each review the experience of the last great depression when jobs are dropping like dead flies – performance is not enough. One must impress everyone around you so that you will be one of the last few standing. To do this, we can learn from the animals in times of drought and famine. The rule of survival of the fittest is truly evident in the animal world during drought and famine. The same can be said for the corporate jungle during times of economic difficulty. The fittest in the corporate jungle are those that know how to impress quickly and are able to perform consistently.

To ensure that you will be one of the fittest and survive, especially if your firm is hurting during these financially unstable markets, you can manage your office politics tactics by modifying them to better suit the changing culture of the office. Changes in the market mandate change for yourself and your firm. For example, if your firm is facing an uptick in profits but a significant overage in workload, you can change your stance to better handle this change (although this might be unusual in our economy today). Or if your office is having a slow-down in the workload and the culture is changing to increase the amount of marketing necessary to win a project, to survive, you must change too.

The same can be said for changes to the political environment in your office. The changes in the economy have caused many managers to become much more hands-on, stripping responsibilities from young professionals in an effort to ensure quality. If you are one of these young professionals, you must change with this change in your office's political culture. If you are one of the managers, you must acknowledge this change in your peers and determine if you will make this change, or if you will buck the system, but either way, you will need to change the behavior you have toward your peers and your young professionals. Any way you look at it, you must modify yourself and your behaviors to deal with a change in the office politics environment around you. But first you must open your mind and understand that you are the only one that can influence your career in such a significant manner. By learning from the animals that change can benefit you, you can become a better office politics player.

By learning from the animals, we can increase the number of tools at our disposal for dealing with office politics and you can increase the chances of survival in the concrete jungle. One way in which you might quickly assess how you should behave would be by following this quick formula of five easy to use animal personas. These five animal methods are an easy way to categorize yourself or your co-workers and better react or predict the way your interactions will play-out.

Tortoise – If you are intent upon avoiding conflict and conscious of other's feelings or concerned about "stepping on someone's toes," the tortoise may be the most appropriate of teachers. This method is appropriate if victory is tentative or out of reach and the conflict is meaningless or trivial. This stance is not one which should be used on a continual basis without long contemplation. By taking on this persona, you may be perceived as taking a disinterested part in your own career. Use of this stance may be wise in some situations, but should be used consistently only with careful caution.

Crocodile – If you know what you desire, aren't afraid to be competitive, have the goal in your sights and don't care if others get in your way, the crocodile may be the animal guide most appropriate for you. This stance should not be used on a continual basis, but may be best used in emergency situations when there are few options. The crocodile is a frightening opponent, and although you may later desire to be perceived as conciliatory, if you have taken the approach of the crocodile for too long, you may always be perceived to be this horrible predator.

Dog – When you are willing to acquiesce to the desires of others and sacrifice your own, the accommodating stance of the dog is appropriate. However, this stance is not one which should be taken on a regular basis and should only be used when an issue is significantly more important to the other party and the relationship you have with them is extremely valuable. Otherwise, this position would only be detrimental to your position. Like the dog, you may be perceived to be loyal only to one person if you continue to capitulate to their desires. When following this method, you might be wiser to keep its use to a minimum. Like the tortoise, you may be perceived to be taking a "back-seat" in your career – a perception to be avoided.


Lion – If you are more interested in finding a solution to partially satisfy all parties, rather than capitulating your own or denying the other party's, the best stance would be that of the lion. However, if the lion stance is to be used, your position must be strong because you must convince everyone to relinquish something in return for the compromise. The lion's stance is one of strength and dominance, which is required to create compromise, both from your partners and your dissenters. If you are leading the way to compromise, the lion's method of leadership is best. This does not mean to be dominating as the lion is with his prey, but rather look to how the lion interacts with its den-mates. Within his pride, the lion leads by binding each lion to him by ensuring that they hunt as a pack and are always fed and their young protected. To keep this pack in working-order the leader must forego pursuit of female lions outside of the pride and hunt with his den-mates, avoiding working alone. If the lion cannot meet the basic needs of feeding the pride and protecting the young, the other lions will become dissenters. By bringing compromise to the table, you must lead in the same manner, creating a reason for someone to follow your lead while giving-up something of yours to show them your sincerity.

Monkey – For those of you which may be seeking a more collaborative approach, the monkey may be the animal guide which you should model your behavior after. By understanding each viewpoint and acknowledging the importance of all parties, you can attempt to find a solution which meets the needs of everyone involved. This type of stance is highly-successful in the long-term for many people. This persona is viewed as a mediator with a strong ability to create "win-win" solutions for delicate situations. If you desire others to see you as a problem-solver and a person with a plan, this may be the best stance for you.

You can apply this formula both through short-term situational views and through long-term views of yourself and others. For example, if you view yourself negatively, but view others in a positive manner, your animal guide should be the bear. However, if you view yourself positively but view others in a negative light, the crocodile would be a more appropriate representation of your views. But if you view both yourself and others negatively, a tortoise is more representative of your stance. And lastly, the monkey represents the views of one which views themselves and others positively.

There are many other animals which may represent your individual stance, but for convenience, these five are the best uses for the quick formula. However, in expounding on this point, if this book were one of those cheesy self-help books we all know and love, at this point, it might say something like: "Imagine yourself as the jungle animals and take from each the lesson that is most valuable for each situation." But this is not a cheesy book, this is truly meant to help, so we broke-down the key "do's" and "do-not's" for each animal for you.

# Key Lessons from animals

| Animal | Key Positive Lessons | Key Negative Lessons |
|---|---|---|
| Chameleon | Changes his complexion according to his environment | Small and unobtrusive, no chameleon will ever show his true colors |
| Cockroach | Developed an exoskeleton of near impregnability and will outlive a nuclear event | Their just gross – how do they even stand each other?! |
| Dinosaurs | Large and strong, they dominated the world for millions of years | Dead because they couldn't adapt to sudden change |
| Monkey | Works in teams and shares among the group; can learn sign language, which is cool | They can only use tools for a limited number of purposes – their ability to learn is stunted |
| Rat | Proliferating across the planet and some places are a healthy snack or lab-tool | Filthy in their natural state and disease carriers (remember that whole black-plague epidemic?!) |
| Dog | Loyal and loving, they will never lose faith in their leader | Loyal to a fault – they will never question their leader |
| Lion | Strong and very territorial, they will protect their den and their homes with voracity – the King of the Jungle | Their leadership system is based on strength alone and not wits or experience |
| Shark | Will attack all of their food head-on and with the same respect | Would sooner bite and kill another shark than share and work in a team to meet a need |
| Crocodile | Will kill only what it can eat and what it is sure it can kill; is a remnant of the dinosaur age and is therefore long-lived | Makes a better shoe or handbag than a neighbor, so have been hunted to near extinction in many parts of the world |
| Beaver | Industrious and hard-working for the entirety of their lives | One storm can wash away several years' work in minutes |
| Bear | Protecting the young is second nature | Napping for half the year allows many other animals to take over their homes in the winter months |
| Snake | Changes skin frequently to reinvent self | Changes skin frequently to reinvent self (no, this is not a typo!) |
| Eagle | Strong and true to their mates and offspring | Unable to cope with environmental changes in diet required due to pesticide proliferation |
| Mustang | A strong leader, with little or no conflict in his nature | Very vulnerable to predators and virtually lost their freedom to humanity's need for conveyance |
| Tortoise | A slow and steady approach will win for him every time | Afraid of conflict, this guy will shrivel-up in his shell before stepping-out on a limb and fighting for his life |
| Panda | Majestic and mesmerizing | Leaving this planet because the human has no ability to stop taking their homes |

Now, notice that no animal is called-out as the perfect example – each has a flaw or weakness. The perfect player simply does not exist. However, as far as we can surmise, the human being is the superior political animal (although were we dinosaurs, we would likely have said the same). Not only do we dominate the world and reshape it to our needs, but we are also very capable of consciously reshaping ourselves to better work within the environment.

However, many of us humans do not do a good job and under-perform based on the expectations of our peers and sometimes even ourselves. And we are also under-performing as a species in our role within the environment. We need to humble ourselves to learn from the animals how to better work within the earth's ecosystem and remember the harmony with it that we once had. However, we should know that we can change and to start that movement, we need to change ourselves first, then lead by example.

*You must not lose faith in humanity. Humanity is an ocean; if a few drops of the ocean are dirty, the ocean does not become dirty.*
*~ Mahatma Gandhi*

Illustration 27

To begin change, the first step is to work within the political machine around you. Acknowledge the personalities and behavior of yourself and those around you, how it might resemble that of our animal brethren, then embrace it. Use your strength and weaknesses to your advantage, then look to those around you and use theirs in the same manner. If you have a young lady on your team that is particularly good at preparing reports and enjoys making them perfect, focus all of your efforts on making sure that she grows that skill into an asset for you. The same goes for your supervisor. If you know that you are better at a particular activity or task than he is, offer to help him complete the next one that comes up.

You are the person that has invested most time and energy in making yourself successful. Only you can stand-up for yourself and be an advocate for your career to ensure success. And one way to ensure success is to become a master-player at the game of office politics. Office politics are not all that bad and can actually prove to be very effective, provided we do not play dirty, we play well and continue to grow. And we know that this game is not unnatural or impossible to play, because the animals play jungle politics every day and do not get played out. Because for the animals, playing their game well is a life and death matter. If they get played out, they ended up on another animal's dining table. So, if you want to be successful and make the changes in your career for the better, remember that the animals can contribute to our political games and you will be well on your way.

www.ingramcontent.com/pod-product-compliance
Lightning Source LLC
Chambersburg PA
CBHW071610170426
43196CB00034B/2285